WOVEN IN FAVOUR

Unconsumed by Fire

A MEMOIR

BY DESDEMONA BENNET

"When thou walkest through the fire, thou shalt not be burned;
neither shall the flame kindle upon thee."
— *Isaiah 43:2 (KJV)*

Melbourne, Australia
2025

Copyright © 2025 by Desdemona Bennet

All rights reserved.

No part of this book may be reproduced, distributed, or transmitted in any form or by any means, including photocopying, recording, or other electronic or mechanical methods, without the prior written permission of the publisher, except in the case of brief quotations embodied in critical reviews or articles.

For permission requests, please contact the publisher at: **desdemona.bennet@gmail.com**

First Edition: 2025

In consideration of the sacredness of memory and privacy, some names and details have been gently altered.

Unless otherwise noted, all Scripture quotations are taken from the **King James Version (KJV)** of the Bible.

DEDICATION

For my father, SP. Your love continues to shape my heart daily, and I speak of you often, for I love you as fiercely in death as I did in life.

For my mother, Catherine. Your wisdom created pathways I could not have dreamed of, and for all who hold onto hope, no matter how impossible the journey may seem.

PREFACE

"For I know the thoughts that I think toward you, saith the Lord, thoughts of peace, and not of evil, to give you an expected end."
—Jeremiah 29:11 (KJV)

From the very beginning, my life has unfolded as a story of grace, filled with both trials and triumphs, shaped by the remarkable people God has placed in my path. Each chapter reflects the undeniable truth of this promise: even when the road ahead felt uncertain or overwhelmingly steep, there was always a plan, a purpose, and a future unfolding beyond what I could see. Waiting to be revealed.

This book is a reflection on the seasons of favour that have grounded me, the transformations that have challenged and stretched me, and the fires that have refined me without consuming my spirit. It's a testament to the faithfulness of a God who tenderly holds each thread of our lives, ensuring that even the tough times are woven into something beautiful.

As you read through the pages, I invite you to walk alongside me through the years. Come and witness the faith that has carried me, the love that has surrounded me, and the lessons that have shaped who I am today. I hope my story will resonate with you, reminding you that, no matter where you find yourself or what obstacles you face, God's plans are always aimed at our good.

ACKNOWLEDGMENTS

To my husband, thank you for loving me and understanding me in ways that don't always need words, even across rooms. For every gentle "Cup of tea, Mary?" that reminded me I wasn't alone in this. You steadied me when I was unsettled and gave me the courage to begin. Your love is a rare and profound blessing, the greatest comfort I treasure.

To our six boys, you colour my days with joy, mischief, and meaning. You stretch my heart in every direction and remind me daily that life is to be lived and worth writing about. You've found your way into every chapter I live. This book was born in the beautiful chaos of being yours. Thank you.

To my friends, your presence is threaded like gold through every fabric of my life.

To Dawn, your gracious patience and expertise skilfully transformed my story from layout to its final form, illuminating its path to find a home in print and beyond.

AUTHOR'S NOTE

This memoir is written under the name Desdemona Bennet, a name borrowed from the glyphs of women who lingered in my imagination. Desdemona from Shakespeare, fierce in loyalty, brave in heart, yet tender in spirit. Elizabeth Bennet from Austen, sharp of wit, fiercely independent, and unwaveringly true. Though the name is borrowed, the story is my own.

TABLE OF CONTENTS

Dedication 3

Preface 4

Acknowledgments 5

Author's Note 6

Part I: Foundations of Grace
Roots of Favour 11
The Village That Raised Me 18
The Pillar Beneath My Story 23
Sayuni A *Silent Song of Grace* 31
Hope, my window to the city's world 34
David *Authority, Power and Reverence* 36
Rejection *The Door to a New Beginning* 39
Phenomenal Maama Sarah *Grace in Motion* 43

Part II: Becoming

The Hill That Raised Us *A world within Budo and Monica*	53
Taibah *A Taste of Liberty*	62
Mpoma School *Toil for Quality and Success*	67
Patrick, my brotherman	71
The End of One Stair, the Start of Another *Namirembe Hillside High School*	74
A Discipline of Becoming	82
Freshvine Bookshop	85
Destiny helper	89
The Moment of Truth	94
Choices *The Hidden Cost of Freedom*	101
The Future Began *Quietly, and in Disguise*	108
When Want Speaks Louder Than Will	112
Ripples from Valentine's Day	115
A Future Forged by Haste and Resolve	118

Part III: Love, Loss, and Becoming More

Marriage, Motherhood, and the Bonds That Sustained Me	125
Born of Two, Held by One	128
Swallowing Pride, Finding a Way	135
A Swift Unfolding and Divine Airwaves	137
A Brief Vacation	141
Graduation	144
Rebuilding on Shifting Ground	146
Caleb	158
Consult Care	160
The Stewardship of Pain	164
Rebuild to tear down?	167
The Weight of Expectations	170
Canaan	180

Everything, Everywhere, All at Once	187
Anchors of Hope	190
A Storm Named 2014	194
Loss, Grief and uncertainty	199

Part IV: A New Land, A New Life

Australia here I come!	215
A City, A Centre, A Second Chance	224
Footscray A *Mini-Africa in Melbourne*	228
Door Knocking for Change	232
Pastor Claude	234
The News I Dreaded	236
Simon and Sarah	244
Trish and Walter	249
The Unconventional Road to BSL	255
Beyond the Impossible	260
Vivian	264
A Mustard Seed	266

PART I:

FOUNDATIONS OF GRACE

ROOTS OF FAVOUR

I was born on Friday, 23 December 1983—or was it 1984?

My father, Simon Peter, ever the doting one, would sometimes say it was 1984—perhaps wanting to keep his "precious baby" a year younger, or maybe his memory of the events surrounding both years had blurred over time. My mother, Catherine, however, would usually confirm—firmly—that it was 1983, often trying to jog his memory by recounting specific events that had occurred on the night of my birth.

It would have been easier if they had left the hospital with a birth certificate, but I don't think official birth certificates were issued at the time—or if they were, well, my mother didn't get one for me at birth. I would only visit the hospital in my teenage years to get a birth note, which I then used to apply for my birth certificate.

I know it's quite an interesting system. But hey, you'd have to be familiar with events in Uganda at the time before judging it. The first documents I saw bearing my name were my baptism card and my health immunisation card.

In hindsight, this early fragmentation in my birth record was perhaps a subtle foreshadowing of how my story would unfold—a life laced with paradoxes, infused with favour and unearned blessings, marred by hardship, yet grounded in divine orchestration.

I would also later read that, around this time, the world that welcomed me was far from serene. On 23 December 1983, chilling news spread: scientists, including Carl Sagan, introduced the concept of "nuclear winter" in a paper warning of global darkness and plummeting temperatures following nuclear explosions. They described how such devastation could block the sun, poison the atmosphere, and endanger all life. It was a stark reminder of human fragility—an extraordinary backdrop for what was otherwise one of many ordinary births in Mulago Hospital that night.

Uganda, at the time, was itself under siege—gripped by the tremors of the Ugandan Bush War, a brutal conflict between the Uganda National Liberation Army (UNLA) and Yoweri Museveni's National Resistance Army (NRA). The haunting legacy of Idi Amin's tyrannical rule (1971–1979) still lingered, and political instability had bled into every facet of life. Families grappled with poverty, uncertainty, and fear as violence tore through communities and trauma loomed over the land.

Despite the turmoil surrounding the country and the uncertainty clouding my origins, I was not born into despair. I was born into hope.

A Precious Baby and Family Dynamics

My parents' choice to bring me into the world was nothing less than a miraculous act of love and faith.

My father, Simon Peter (SP), was born in 1925. He was a man of depth—his life was shaped by resilience, resourcefulness, humility, discipline, an unshakable sense of duty, and a quiet pursuit of excellence. He belonged to what many call the Greatest Generation. By the time I was born, he was already 58 years old. His life experiences had moulded him into a pillar of strength and wisdom. His steadfast commitment to family, faith, and integrity reflected the enduring values of his time, leaving an indelible mark on those fortunate enough to know him.

My mother, Catherine, was born in 1939, part of what is now referred to as the Silent Generation—a cohort shaped by the austerity of wartime and the hopefulness of the post-war boom. Renowned for their resilience, strong work ethic, and commitment to family, they navigated a world rapidly changing yet rooted in traditional values. She possessed a quiet strength, sharp discernment, and a grace that left an impression without ever demanding attention. Her love for God had anchored her long before she met my father. She walked in wisdom, carried herself with gentleness, and loved with intention. By the time I came into the world, she was 44 years old—a grown woman in every sense—embodying the calm resilience and steady grace that defined her generation. Her life stood as a testament to an era where actions spoke louder than words, and a person's worth was measured not by declarations, but by the consistency of their deeds.

Before marrying my mother on December 29, 1982, my father was a widower. He had lost his first wife, Tabisa, in 1978. However, their story—and the cultural values that shaped it—goes beyond this simple fact. Following Ankole tradition, my father married Tabisa after the death of her first husband, who was his brother, Kabwinda. This wasn't a love story in the romantic sense; it was a bond formed out of duty and a deep-rooted cultural commitment to maintaining family connections and heritage.

Among the Banyankole, it was customary—and often expected—for a man to take in the widow of his late brother, especially when children were involved. The idea wasn't to replace a husband but to preserve the family structure and ensure that children were not left vulnerable or disconnected from their roots. In this case, it was about George, Tabisa's son from her first marriage. By marrying her, SP wasn't just honouring his brother's memory; he was safeguarding his nephew's future. It was a way of saying: that you are still one of us, and we will not let you fall through the cracks.

Such arrangements were less about personal desire and more about collective responsibility—about stepping in where life had left a void, and about docking the family through transitions that might otherwise tear it apart.

Together, SP and Tabisa raised nine children. George was the eldest—technically SP's nephew but raised as his son—and he was followed by Mary, Keziah, David, Daniel, Ruth, Enoch, Elizabeth, and Damalie (also known as Sandra).

My mother, Catherine, meanwhile, had been living a very different life. She was an independent single mother raising her son, Patrick, who was born in October 1964. Much of her young adulthood was spent in Kampala, where she worked as a nurse at Mulago Hospital—beginning in her early twenties.

There's something almost poetic about the fact that I was eventually born in that very same hospital, where she had served for many years.

Patrick once told me that when he started high school, my mother felt her maternal duty had reached a pivotal milestone. She had done her part as a single mother. So, she dropped him off at an all-boys boarding school near her ancestral home in western Uganda, resigned from her job, and returned home to care for her ageing parents—especially her beloved father.

But that season of respite was short-lived. The *Tukutendereza* fellowship, guided by their collective wisdom—what they call *omusana*—determined that it was time for my father to remarry. As Scripture teaches, "And the Lord God said, it is not good that the man should be alone; I will make him an help meet for him."

—Genesis 2:18 (KJV), and so, on spiritual grounds, the fellowship entered into prayer. In time, SP married Catherine.

In doing so, he added to his already-large family—receiving Patrick, and soon after, me.

For my mother, this union was an act of obedience and self-sacrifice. It was far removed from the idyllic love stories many imagine. Her life, as she knew it, was about to change irrevocably.

The circumstances surrounding their union were steeped in deep faith. The blending of two families—each with its own history, dynamics, and emotional weight—came with inevitable challenges. And yet, what emerged was a profound display of love, resilience, and commitment.

Their faith became the cornerstone—the unshakable anchor they would lean on to hold them steady through all that life would bring. And oh yes, life would bring a great deal. Unexpected turns, seasons of testing, and moments of triumph lay ahead. But through it all, they would return to that foundation of trust in God's plan.

When I was born, my parents received me as a gift from God—a sign of new beginnings. I was their "precious baby," a source of joy, comfort, and companionship in their later years. My arrival, in many ways, filled a space that only a child born into such a union could. I became a thread of connection, weaving together the different parts of their lives, offering not just presence—but purpose.

Their faith was anchored in the East African Revival, a spiritual awakening that took hold in the 1930s and coursed through Uganda, Rwanda, Kenya and beyond with enduring strength. Locally, it became known as Tukutendereza—"we praise you"—or Bazukufu, "the Reawakened." The chorus Tukutendereza Yesu rang out in those days like a banner of joy and surrender. First sung during the revival's early stirrings, it filled cathedrals, mission halls and open fields. For many, it was more than a song; it was a declaration of new life, often following moments of deep repentance or testimony. This dynamic movement is believed to have sprung from the global Pentecostal fire that began at Azusa Street in Los Angeles (1906-1915) and was marked by radical public confession of sin, unity across tribes, denominations and nations, and a fervent call to walk in the light (1 John 1:7). My parents belonged fully to this reawakened fellowship—true Bazukufu in every sense. Word and walk.

As their child, I was born into this life of devotion—automatically a *mulokole*, a "saved one." I began attending their weekly gatherings as soon as I could walk, and to this day, my mother remains an active member.

I grew up listening to my parents' testimonies—over and over again. Whether at the family prayer altar every evening at 5 p.m., during early morning prayers at 5 a.m., on evangelism missions, or when we welcomed visitors into our home, their voices filled the air with stories of faith. Every Wednesday at 6 p.m., we gathered for communal fellowship with fellow *balokole*. The atmosphere would swell with the soulful, repetitive singing of *Tukutendereza*—a chorus of praise to God—followed by worship, testimonies, and teatime.

Day after day, week after week, I heard my parents testify to their salvation. In later years, when my father was canonised, I would quietly recite his testimony whenever he spoke publicly or preached. For my parents, the revival was more than just a historical event; it was their very way of life—a living, breathing mission.

Their orthodoxy shaped their outlook on everything—family, relationships, community, and daily life. Scripture guided their every decision, with verses not only memorised but etched deep in their hearts and lived out in the routines of our home.

Growing up, I experienced love and discipline in equal measure. My father was a man of deep faith and warmth. He told the best stories, full of wisdom and humour, and had a way of making even ordinary things feel important. He loved me deeply, and I never once doubted that. But he also believed in shaping character. He corrected me with gentleness, never harshness, always wanting me to understand, not just obey. He taught me that honesty mattered, that you don't make promises you can't keep, and that how you treat people says more about you than anything else.

My mother, on the other hand, spoke less—but when she did, you listened. Often, she didn't need to say a word. One look from her was enough to straighten you out. She carried the kind of authority that didn't announce itself. A typical African mother: firm, watchful, and always ten steps ahead. She kept everything running, mostly in silence, but her presence was constant. She led by doing. We didn't talk about discipline—we lived it.

Together, they raised me on simple but steady values—faith in God, respect for others, and a sense of purpose that comes from knowing who you are and what you stand for. Their love gave me roots. Their example gave me direction. And their faith shaped how I began to see the world—not as something to survive, but something to grow into.

By now, it's clear that by the time I arrived, my family was already well-established. From my father's side came nine young adults, and from my mother's side, Patrick, her firstborn son. I was the latecomer—the baby born after everyone else had long since left the crib. This made for a complex, yet deeply rich upbringing—one coloured by stories, layered perspectives, and silent expectations.

In many ways, I was born into a village of discipline and God-fearing tradition.

And in our family's narrative, Tabisa's legacy—the woman who raised those nine children—remains a thread interwoven with honour and remembrance.

THE VILLAGE THAT RAISED ME

From birth to age six, I don't recall living anywhere for an extended period except our home in Bweyale village, located in the Mawogola sub-county of what is now Sembabule district. At the time, it was still considered part of Masaka district.

I do, however, remember staying for a while with my late sister Kezia and her family in Nkeika, several miles from home. Kezia ran a nursery school at her home, which served the local community—and I attended, alongside her youngest daughter, Agatha. Both Kezia and her husband, George, were respected educators. Though I'm not entirely sure, I believe George served as headmaster of a local primary or secondary school in the area for many years.

I have fond memories of visiting my maternal grandparents in Kiringa, where I had the chance to meet my extended family—cousins, uncles, aunts, and their children. My memories of this time are somewhat vague now, but I've pieced together many stories over the years, especially during visits to my grandmother after my grandfather passed away. In later years, I would often accompany my mother to see her, which helped me learn more about our family history and connections.

Our home in Bweyale was a sanctuary of both abundance and simplicity. We lived with my paternal grandmother, *Kaaka* Maryamu

Babota. She was the heart of the homestead —a graceful, wise woman of advancing years who was deeply respected in the community. She carried herself with an elegance that seemed to fill the air with warmth. Her ever-present smile endeared her to everyone—though perhaps none more than her beloved son, my father.

Kaaka had endured considerable hardship in her life. After losing her husband, my grandfather Nziriga, at a young age, she raised five boys on her own. It was a life shaped by sacrifice and the quiet strength that so often defines women of her generation.

Among her sons, a special bond had blossomed between her and my father. Their closeness was apparent to everyone who witnessed their interactions. Whether in the easy laughter they shared, the small affectionate exchanges between them, or a deeper connection beyond words, I always sensed that my father held a unique place in her heart.

In later years, I would come to understand that this deep bond between *Kaaka* and my father likely stemmed from the pivotal role he played in introducing Christianity to the family. That spiritual foundation earned him not only her admiration but also widespread respect and reverence as a leader—both within the household and the wider community. His faith shaped his life and deeply influenced ours, laying the groundwork for a legacy that would endure across generations.

Kaaka's love was a blessing woven into the very fabric of my childhood.

She shielded me during my early years from the firmer hand of my parents. Despite my place in the family, I was not a particularly docile child. I was imaginative, often restless, and occasionally defiant. Whenever mischief was brewing, *Kaaka* was the one who calmly diffused the tension.

My favourite kind of mischief? Playing outside for hours on end—and, of course, feeding my cup of milk to the cat instead of drinking it. I didn't like milk then, and I still don't. But in a pastoralist family, there was no escaping it. Thankfully, the cat was my faithful accomplice.

I remember how many times my parents would have to call me—over and over—before I responded. Everything else seemed more interesting than whatever they wanted me to do. But I'm sure you can relate; at that age, attention is fleeting, and the world outside always feels more urgent than any adult's instructions.

While the memories between one and six years old remain mostly hazy, those early moments of peace and affection with her during my formative years shaped the foundation of my childhood. She wasn't just a grandmother; she was a pillar—quietly holding everything together, teaching me the value of love, patience, and grace in the simplest moments.

My brother Enock and his wife Joy lived in the same compound with us for a time before eventually moving to their own home just a few kilometres away. One memory from that season stands out—one I've never forgotten. When Joy gave birth to their first child, Sharon, I went over to visit the newborn. In a moment of excitement, Joy asked what name we should give her.

Without hesitation, I named her *Mpoyogoma*—which, in my mind, meant "Lion."

The word I intended was *Mpologoma*, the proper word for "lion" in our language. But I was still learning to speak and had a lisp, thanks to the gap between my teeth. Certain sounds—especially s and z—came out as a soft "th." So *Mpoyogoma* it was.

I can't say why I chose "Lion" for her. Maybe it was because she was a plump baby. Or perhaps it was something else entirely. After all, a child's imagination is a wondrous and boundless thing, where reality and fantasy often blend. Strangely, I had never seen a lion in real life—nor had I watched one on television, let alone that moving pictures could come through a box. And yet, there she was—a lioness with a name that seemed to come from somewhere beyond reason, shaped by the pure, unfiltered creativity of a child's heart.

Looking back, maybe the image came from the folklore my mother and Kaaka used to tell—those quiet evening stories in which animals spoke and the world felt bigger, more magical, and somehow closer to my little heart.

Next to our homestead lived my father's youngest brother, Ncunda, whom we called Uncle Nguna. He lived there with his wife Joyce and their two young sons at the time—Muhoozi, who was just a couple of years younger than me, and his baby brother, Mugume. Uncle Nguna was the youngest of Kaaka's sons. They were Kabwinda, Kamugabo, SP, Tamwesigire, and finally—him, Ncunda—the last in a line of brothers who significantly shaped our family's life and legacy.

Uncle Nguna also had two older daughters, Rose and Hope, from a previous relationship. They were closer in age to my older siblings, and by the time I came into the picture, both were already young adults living their own lives in the city. My connection with them, while familial, felt more like that of a younger niece than a peer.

In time, Joyce gave birth to two more girls, completing their growing family. But by then, I was already growing older and beginning to engage more deeply with life beyond the immediate folds of our homestead. As a result, my connection with those youngest cousins wasn't as strong. My memories of them remain hazy—like distant melodies, I once heard but never fully learned the words to. They belonged to a chapter of family life that was gently unfolding around me, yet just beyond the borders of my childhood awareness.

What I do remember clearly, though, are the details of our day-to-day life—the simple, tightly knit existence we shared in that communal setting. And as surprising as it may sound, by the time I was six years old, I had never seen my reflection in a mirror. I had no real concept of what I looked like. My image of myself came entirely from the faces around me—the way my father looked at me, the affection in my mother's eyes, and Kaaka's protective embrace. These expressions, more than anything else, told me who I was.

In this communal homestead, life wasn't built on personal space or possessions but on shared rhythms, inherited customs, and unspoken responsibilities. Everything was done together—cooking, storytelling, fetching water, even sleeping. There was no vanity mirror in the corner or private time for self-observation. What mattered most was the rhythm of daily life, belonging, and the unshakable sense that your identity was mirrored in the people who surrounded you.

THE PILLAR BENEATH MY STORY

My father was greatness personified. If I were to attempt to fully capture his essence, I might never find the space to tell my own story. He was broader, deeper, and more profound in every way than anything I have ever known. He remains, to this day, the most significant presence in my life. He often said there are three kinds of people in this world: those who think, those who don't, and those for whom others do the thinking. It wasn't just a clever saying—it was how he understood people and moved through the world. And when he spoke, you couldn't help but want to be among the first kind.

Those who think, he said, are steady. They see the bigger picture, weigh their steps, and think past the moment. They don't panic. They don't flail. They navigate life like a person walking with a lamp in their hand—able to see just far enough ahead not to fall into every ditch. They don't avoid every hardship, but they don't walk into trouble blind either.

Those who don't think are different. They stand at the crossroads, not knowing whether to go left or right. They drift, move with the crowd, and wait for life to decide for them. Not because they lack the ability, but because they've never stopped long enough to ask themselves where they're going—or why.

But the third kind—those for whom others think—he believed they were the most at risk. They surrender their choices to louder voices. They walk in shoes they didn't choose, down roads they never questioned. And by the time they realise it, they're often too far gone to turn back. "Never become the one they think for," he would say. "Because when someone else is doing your thinking, they're also shaping your future."

Some truths don't settle in the heart until they've travelled with you through pain. Like they say back home: *Ngu akati kukakucumita omumaisho, kati wheeza*—only when the stick has poked your eye do you finally open it wide. Warnings don't make you wise. Only walking and experiencing life does. And when the thorns come, as they always do, the words you once heard return—no longer as advice, but as lived truth. By then, you're not the same person who first heard them. You've been shaped by the very path you didn't yet understand.

I loved him deeply, but I also revered him. No major decision in my life was ever made without first seeking his wisdom and weighing his counsel. One day, I will return to tell his story and honour this extraordinary man in the way he truly deserves—or at least try.

He was a towering figure of faith, revered and deeply loved by all who knew him. There was a quiet simplicity about him, yet an undeniable presence that kept you from ever becoming too familiar. His dignity did not demand respect—it simply evoked it. His name alone could light up faces with warmth and admiration.

He wasn't just a "good man" in the polite, posthumous sense of the word. He was genuinely good—through and through, in life and death. Even now, his name carries that same reverence and inspires the same respect and love among all who knew him, or even just heard of him.

Beyond being a son, husband, father, grandfather, friend, and elder, he was a lay priest in the local church he helped establish. A preacher, a church planter in various regions, and the trusted treasurer who carefully managed church finances. His generosity was legendary—always matched by his humility.

He would donate something valuable to the church—sometimes a bull, a cow, or even the finest produce from his garden, like bunches of bananas or baskets of ripe fruit. When these were auctioned to raise funds and the proceeds fell short of what was needed, he would quietly top up the difference from his own pocket. This became such a known gesture that people began to say, "*Simon will top up the balance.*" Whether it was for the church or the wider community, he gave freely, with a heart as open as his hands.

My father was the most hardworking man I knew. Growing up, I can't recall a single morning when he wasn't the first to rise. Long before the rest of us stirred, he would be up—quietly slipping out to milk the cows and see them off with the herdsman. We didn't have many cows then, but you'd think he was tending a whole herd by the care and consistency he gave them.

Afterwards, he'd head straight to his banana garden, where he worked steadily until around one in the afternoon. Then he'd come home for a quick lunch, take a brief rest, and by late afternoon, he'd be off again—this time to his most treasured place: the coffee plantation.

Our home was surrounded by coffee. To say my father took pride in that plantation would be an understatement. It wasn't just a field—it was a sanctuary. The plantation stretched in neat rows of coffee trees, bordered by an abundance of fruit-bearing plants: mango, guava, passionfruit, pawpaw, pineapple, mandarin, avocado, jackfruit, orange, and grapefruit. Each tree felt like a chapter in the story of his life, every branch bearing witness to the richness of what he had built with his hands and heart.

When we picked the coffee beans, there was never a shortage of fruit to enjoy between the work. The air hung heavy with the sweet scent of ripe mangoes and guavas. The ground was often scattered with fallen fruit—soft, fragrant, and waiting to be tasted. It was where labour and reward walked hand in hand, where even the most ordinary task felt like a quiet celebration of the land's generosity.

This plantation wasn't just a source of income. It was a living testament to the quiet harmony between discipline and nature. My father worked the land with purpose, and the land responded in kind—offering more than just crops. It gave beauty, nourishment, and joy.

It wasn't unusual for people to stop by at any time of day, hoping to purchase some of his prized coffee. His beans had a reputation—carefully grown, hand-picked, and full of flavour. But those who came on Sundays soon learnt that business would not be conducted then.

My father was unwavering in his belief that Sundays were for rest. No matter how many buyers came knocking, he never compromised. Sunday was sacred—a day set aside for worship, slow meals, laughter, and simply being together. In the absence of phones, word of mouth was the thread that held the community together. In our neighbourhood, it was well known: Sunday at our home was a day for the soul, not for trade.

And so it was—a life shaped by quiet routines, sacred rhythms, and a land that flourished under the watchful, loving hands of a man who believed in tending things: the soil, the spirit, and everything in between.

All millennials and Gen Y's like me, who were born and raised in remote villages, understand the old-school rhythm of "tell so-and-so to tell so-and-so" that something had happened. And then off you'd go—on foot, or if you were lucky, by bicycle.

The most important announcements, especially death notices, were broadcast on Radio Uganda—the only station we had at the time. There was a fixed hour for news and obituaries, and if you missed it, you simply had to wait until the next top-of-the-hour bulletin.

And to all the Gen Z's and Gen Alphas out there—yes, there really was a time when there were no phones, no iPads, nothing digital. Shocking, I know!

An interesting fact about my father: though he was a Muhima from the Baranzi clan of Ankole—people traditionally known for their pastoralist lifestyle—he was more widely known as a dedicated father and husband, and a renowned coffee farmer with some of the finest beans in the area. But perhaps more uniquely, he was known as Oweishemwe (brethren) Simon and affectionately referred to as "Mulokole dala dala"—the truly saved or born-again one. It was a term used with humour but also deep respect, capturing his unwavering commitment to salvation. When he said "owa highest," meaning of the highest, he meant it with complete sincerity—aspiring to the purest and most elevated form of faith, a goal he pursued with steady devotion. For him, faith, family, and farming were not just values; they were the very fabric of his life. He lived fully in both the spiritual and practical realms.

The Ankole long-horned cattle are held in the highest regard—symbols of honour, dignity, and respect in our community. We are the cattle people. Cows do no wrong.

A man's status is not only measured by how many cows he has, but by how striking they are. Their health, their colouring, the unique patterns on their bodies—all of it speaks to their beauty and value. A truly beautiful cow can stop you in your tracks. Each one is a living reflection of its owner's dignity, care, and standing.

Giving someone a cow is considered the ultimate gift. During weddings and other big celebrations, you'll often hear someone say "*nakuha ente*"—"I've given you a cow." It's not said lightly. It carries weight, meaning, and a sense of permanence that no other gift quite holds. It means you've given something of real substance, something that matters.

When someone cares deeply or wishes you well, they might say "*katungye ente*"—a blessing that you may have cows. Or "*namate*"—"it is like milk"—to describe something too beautiful for words, whether it's a moment, a person, or even a beloved wife. These aren't just sayings— they are part of who we are. This deep connection to cattle runs through us like blood.

However, despite being born into a culture where cattle were central, my father defied tradition in a quiet but significant way. As a Muhima, he was expected to manage impressive herds and build his legacy around them. And while he did have his fair share—enough to earn respect and honour in the eyes of our people—he chose a different path. He poured his energy into farming, particularly coffee.

In a region where coffee was deeply valued but not commonly championed by men of his heritage, his choice might have seemed unusual. But to him, it wasn't about breaking away—it was about building something meaningful with his own hands. Coffee, with its patience and precision, became his signature.

He never abandoned the values of his ancestry—he simply expanded them. My father's decision to focus on coffee farming showcased his ability to adapt to changing times. It also revealed his resourcefulness and creativity, as he managed to build a life that bridged the distance between cultural tradition and modernity. His choice reflected a deeper calling—one not driven by material wealth but by faith and service to God. While the traditional emphasis on cattle still held great significance, my father found purpose in nurturing the land, contributing to the livelihood of our family, and supporting his community through his farming efforts.

My father was a man far ahead of his time, a visionary whose principles were shaped by both his faith and his deep convictions about human dignity. In the 1950s, 60s and 70s, many families in our community, the Bahima, adhered to traditional customs where daughters were married off in exchange for bride price, typically paid in cattle by the suitor's family. Cattle, the currency of wealth in our culture, was seen as a form of payment for the daughter's hand in marriage. Sons were valued for their ability to expand the family's herds and legacy. Daughters, though deeply cherished, were often seen as bridges to prosperity, honoured through the tradition of bride price, which brought cattle and, with it, respect to the family.

But my father, grounded in his faith in God, viewed his children as a sacred gift. He believed that his role as a parent was to nurture and protect them, not to sell them off for material gain. His faith led him to reject the practice of accepting the bride price. He would tell suitors that he was not interested in cows, any sort of gifts or any material wealth, but rather in their promises to love, care for, and protect his daughters. His heart was set on the values of love and respect, which he believed were far more valuable than any earthly possessions.

He would often remind us that his true wealth was not in the cows or land he owned but, in the treasures, stored in heaven. This belief shaped how he raised us and how he viewed his children— not as property to be sold, but as divine blessings entrusted to him by God. His refusal to engage in the practice of bride price was a testament to his deep spirituality and his desire to honour the worth of his children as gifts from God, not items to be exchanged for material wealth.

Though my father did not place the same emphasis on cattle as some of our wealthier neighbours, who often boasted herds numbering in the hundreds or even thousands, we still had enough to feel connected to our heritage. We kept Ankole long-horned cows, though they were never the central focus of our lives. As a child, I drank milk often, and perhaps too much—though I didn't always appreciate it. Milk was an essential part of life in our community, and it was hard to escape it. Ironically, as an adult, milk has become one of my least favourite things, a curious turn given how much I was forced to consume in my youth. But that's the nature of tradition—its influence lingers, even when we try to move beyond it.

SAYUNI
A Silent Song of Grace

In August 1987, my sister, the one who would mark the final chapter of my parents' childbearing years and forever hold the title of the youngest in our family, was born. They named her Sayuni, the Runyakore translation of the word "Zion." For my parents, the name held profound spiritual significance—a symbol of the heavenly Jerusalem, God's eternal kingdom, and the ultimate home of peace and hope for the faithful. Sayuni's arrival, however, came with its own set of challenges. Born with Down syndrome, her presence brought both joy and unique demands on my aging parents. Her developmental delays also meant that the envisioned role of a playmate for me was not to be. Instead, I found myself stepping into a supportive role, helping my parents care for her with the tenderness and patience that her condition required. Sayuni was completely non-verbal, relying on others for nearly every aspect of daily life—feeding, toileting, dressing, bathing, grooming, and more. In her early years, she had learned to walk and often made her way independently to the outdoor kitchen, which stood just a short distance from the main house—a small yet meaningful expression of her autonomy. But this independence was fleeting.

She was deeply unsettled by the sound of rain striking the iron sheet roof of the kitchen. The loud, relentless noise seemed to overwhelm her senses, triggering bouts of anxiety. Whenever the first raindrops fell, she would instinctively dart back to the main house for comfort. One afternoon, I remember vividly, she ran as usual to escape the rain. But this time, she tripped and suffered a devastating fall. From that day forward, Sayuni would never walk again. Her world became confined indoors, her mobility limited to occasional, assisted ventures outside to sunbathe. Watching her spend the remainder of her life in such isolation was profoundly heartbreaking—a life curtailed by both circumstance and fragility. It was a sorrowful reality that weighed heavily on all of us who loved her.

In some families, the challenges of raising a child with a disability are compounded by the harsh realities of societal ignorance and vulnerability. For my family, this reality struck me with painful clarity. I shall mention that her disability was viewed by my parents as a test of faith. Sayuni was kept away from the public eye, not only because of the stigma associated with her condition but also because of a profound fear for her safety.

In our community, it was sadly not uncommon for children with disabilities—especially those unable to speak or advocate for themselves—to be exploited or violated. My parents lived with a constant, deep fear that if harm ever came her way, she would have no way to express her pain or name the perpetrator. And this fear wasn't unfounded. People like my sister were often seen as easy targets in a world that could be unkind and unsafe.

Their decision to limit her exposure wasn't born of shame or rejection but of fierce love and the overwhelming weight of responsibility. They longed to protect her from dangers she couldn't understand, let alone defend herself against. Still, it was a heartbreaking trade-off—shielding her came at the cost of connection, and the solitude that followed often felt like another kind of loss. It was sad.

She never went to school or learned to read or write. She remained entirely dependent on others, especially my mother.

Everyone went about their routines while she remained confined to a room. It was as if life continued on the outside, while hers stood still.

Now and then, my nieces and nephews would visit during the school holidays, usually with their parents—my siblings. But even then, family gatherings were rare. The age differences between us were significant, which made it hard to truly connect. It was uncommon for the entire family to be together under one roof. I can barely recall a Christmas where we were all present. My older siblings had their own families, homes, and responsibilities, and life often pulled us in different directions. The moments we shared were cherished, but they were few and far between.

HOPE, MY WINDOW TO THE CITY'S WORLD

There are many memories from my childhood that have stayed with me, but some you just can't forget—the kind where every detail remains sharp, no matter how much time passes. One of those memories is of my niece, Hope, my sister Elizabeth's daughter, who would come to stay with us during the holidays. Hope was only about two years older than me, and in many ways, she was the perfect sister. I eagerly awaited her visits, counting down the days until she would come. Living in Kampala with her mother, Hope's visits were always the most anticipated moments of the year, bringing with them a sense of joy and excitement. When I would hear about the day she may be coming, I would stay alert, listening for the sound of cars passing by, our home being so close to the main road. In those years, there weren't many cars passing through our village, so the sound of an approaching vehicle was a cause for excitement. When Hope would arrive, the merry-making would start there and then. That night, there would be no sleeping as we would talk each other's ears off! Hope would endeavour to teach me English words, asking me to repeat them, and though I would try my best, I'm sure I sounded like a jumble of mispronunciations. She'd tell me stories about her life in the big city, music, television, and electricity which to me were all foreign concepts, things I could hardly imagine.

The time Hope spent with me was filled with endless games and laughter, running around the homestead, full of energy and joy. Our games would always leave my grandmother feeling anxious—her worry about the constant bustle of activity and the noise of our youthful chatter was palpable. Yet, to me, Hope was not just my niece; she was my sister, my closest friend, my confidant. But all the fun would inevitably end when she had to return to Kampala. The goodbyes were always bittersweet—an adios until the next holiday, until the next time she would come.

DAVID
Authority, Power and Reverence

The second memory that stands out is of my older brother, David—a man of great stature, both within our family and across the country. Now a retired military General, he was a figure equally admired and feared. Back then, he was a Major, though I didn't fully understand the weight of the title. What I did know was that he carried authority and power in a way that left a lasting impression on everyone. His very name commanded awe, and his presence carried an aura of dominance that made him larger than life.

David's visits to our home were events unto themselves, filled with a palpable sense of anticipation. When he would stop by, often on his way to his country home a few miles away, his arrival was heralded by the unmistakable sound of his convoy approaching. The rumble of five or more Land Rovers, packed with soldiers in full uniform—guns, batons, and all the trappings of military order—created a scene of awe-inspiring spectacle. As the convoy wound its way through the village, the disciplined precision of the soldiers left everyone in silent reverence.

Long before the vehicles reached our home, the excitement would have already spread. Villagers would gather near our house, eager to greet the "son of the soil" and witness the momentous occasion of his arrival. By the time David stepped out of his vehicle, the air was electric with a mix of admiration and expectation. True to his generous nature, he would hand out cash to those who greeted him, a gesture that further cemented his reputation as a man of the people. Later, the village would come alive with celebration. The local pubs filled with laughter and cheer as stories of David's visit were retold, and his goodwill became the cause for communal joy. For us, his family, his arrival carried a mix of emotions. I was in awe of him but also slightly terrified. While most children would run to him, shouting "Uncle! Uncle!" I would hesitate, fumbling over how to address him. Occasionally, I too called him "Uncle David," to which he'd laugh warmly and say, "No, call me David."

Despite his approachable moments, his commanding presence always left a lasting impression on me. There were times I'd hear the convoy approaching and quickly hide under the bed, overcome by a childlike fear of the unknown. Yet, in those moments of both trepidation and admiration, I couldn't help but feel proud to be his sibling. David's visits were a reminder of the power he wielded and the respect he commanded, not just as a military leader but as a brother whose larger-than-life persona brought the village to a standstill. For a child like me, those visits were a mix of wonder, excitement, and the thrill of being close to someone who, to us all, seemed almost mythical. Though years have passed, and the grandeur of those moments has faded into history, the essence of who he was to us then—both as a towering figure in the nation and a cherished brother—continues to resonate. The wonder I felt as a child has transformed into admiration as an adult, as I now fully appreciate the sacrifices, discipline, and sense of responsibility that defined him. David's legacy isn't just in the power he commanded or the celebrations that followed his visits, but in the way he connected with people, both his family and the community.

Even now, I smile when I recall the nervous excitement of hearing the convoy in the distance or the pride I felt when villagers gathered to celebrate his homecoming. Those moments were not just about David; they were about belonging, family, and the unspoken bond that tied us all together. To this day, those memories remind me of the rich fabric of our shared life and the extraordinary people who shaped it.

"And we know that all things work together for good to them that love God, to them who are the called according to his purpose."
—Romans 8:28 (KJV)

REJECTION
The Door to a New Beginning

I started my primary education at a local school near the village, but my mother quickly realised it wasn't going to work out for me in that setting. Having been born to him in his advanced years, my father loved me with the indulgence one might show a grandchild. He doted on me endlessly, allowing me much leeway and often turning a blind eye to my playful, unserious attitude toward school. My mother, ever perceptive and determined believed I needed more than what the local schools could offer. She decided that I should be sent to Kampala for my education, recognising that I needed more structure and opportunity. After many discussions, my father reluctantly agreed—despite his deep hesitation about being separated from me, from home, from the environment I knew and had grown up in, and from his care—to let me go to Kampala, a land far away. He wasn't sure it was the right decision, but he trusted my mother's plan enough to let me try.

My sister Mary, her husband Stephen, and their five children lived in King's College Budo, an institution that exuded prestige and grandeur, renowned for its academic excellence and historical significance, a beacon of success and opportunity in those days and continues to this day. The college had a junior school—Budo Junior School—an extension of King's College Budo, serving as the primary section of the school. This was where my father thought I would thrive. My sister's younger children at the time, the twins Mercy and Timothy attended the junior school, and he imagined that we would be buddies, walking and studying together, easing the transition into this new world.

Although I had not grown up alongside my nieces Patience, Charity and Mercy or my nephews Paul and Timothy, who were all much older than me, they were still young enough to guide me and help me navigate the ways of this new life. My father believed this would be an opportunity for us to bond while I also received a city education, and my mother agreed. Preparations quickly took shape for the move.

The day came sooner than I expected, and I wasn't ready. I was dressed, my small suitcase packed and placed in the trunk of my father's purple 1977 Toyota Corona. We were going to Kampala. A new chapter was beginning, though I didn't know what it would look like.

It was a long drive. I had never been that far from home before. I looked out of the window as trees and bushes flew past us. It felt strange—watching the road stretch on and on, the land unfamiliar. I had grown up in one place, and now we were heading somewhere I didn't know. Everything was moving quickly, yet inside I felt still, quiet.

As we got closer to the city, the sights changed. There were more houses, more cars, and people everywhere. I noticed the noise, the buildings. Everything looked bigger, faster. I stared at it all, taking it in. Kampala was not what I had known. It was different in every way.

When we arrived, things changed quickly. My mother had arranged for me to stay with Mary and her family, and my father had agreed to the plan. But when we got there, she said no. She told them there was no space for me. That I would teach her children bad manners from the village. She said I couldn't stay.

My father didn't say anything. He just sat there, quiet, his eyes heavy. I could tell he was disappointed. My mother said nothing either. Her face was calm, but I knew she felt it. I didn't understand everything, but I felt the rejection. The sadness. The silence between them.

These words were spoken in my presence to my parents, in my mother tongue, and make no mistake, I understood exactly what had just happened. My sister had rejected me. I hadn't made sense of much at that moment, but I clearly remember the words *emicwe mibi*—bad manners—repeated over and over in my head as she said them. The phrase stuck with me like an unwelcome thorn. As I sat there, a silent witness to this new world around me, the weight of what had been said settled in. I wondered, what was going to happen now? Were we going to go back home, to the village where I could see my *Kaaka* and my friends from the local school?

I found myself utterly out of place—like a fish out of water. The world around me felt foreign in contrast to the simple life I had always known. I recalled the stories Hope used to share whenever she returned home for the holidays from Kampala, painting vivid pictures of a life so different from mine. And now, here I was, thrust into that very world, struggling to find my footing in a reality that felt like it belonged to someone else. As I sat there sheepishly, I couldn't shake the question lingering in my mind—what *micwe mibi* (bad manners) did I have? Had I already broken some unspoken rule? Was I too naïve, too unsophisticated for this place? The thought gnawed at me, making me even more aware of how different I was from everything and everyone in this environment. But what unsettled me even more was that these words came from someone I barely knew—someone with whom I had never shared a personal interaction. She had never spent Christmas or holidays at home, at least not in any way I could remember. Perhaps there had been a few brief visits, an hour here or there, but nothing significant enough to leave an impression. I knew her only by name and by the fact that she was my sister. So why would she say this? Why would she label me in such a harsh, definitive way?

That moment marked the beginning of a pondering that would stretch across the years, lingering in my thoughts and heart. Why the rejection? Why the hurtful words? At that moment, I had no answers—just the cold sting of being unwelcomed in a world I had hoped to embrace. It wasn't a simple disappointment; it was the beginning of a journey where I would wrestle with the complexities of family, identity, and belonging. The pieces of this puzzle wouldn't start to come together for years, and even now, some of the answers still elude me.

* * *

PHENOMENAL MAAMA SARAH
Grace in Motion

After that conversation, we didn't stay much longer. As I mentioned before, my mother, with her forward-thinking nature and unwavering resolve about my education, already had a Plan B. I can't say for certain if this contingency had been in her mind all along or if it arose out of necessity from what had just transpired. Whatever the case, I remain deeply grateful to be her daughter. Over the years, many who have come to know me, describe my resolve as unyielding when I decide on something—a trait I now realise I inherited from her.

As I had shared earlier, my mother had spent years in Kampala, carving out a life for herself in a city that promised opportunities to those with ambition and determination. As a young girl, she had left the village behind, seeking a future that stretched beyond the limits of rural life. Her education, though modest, had opened doors and led her to Mulago Hospital—then the largest and most prestigious referral hospital in the country—where she built her career as a nurse. She understood firsthand the transformative power of education and opportunity, and she was determined that

I, too, would have the chance to rise beyond the limitations of our beginnings.

During her time in the city, my mother formed a deep and enduring friendship with Maama Sarah, a fellow member of the *Tukutendereza* fellowship. Their bond had been forged years earlier when they were neighbours, united by their shared faith and determination to create better lives for their families. As it is often said, God's plans are laid out even before we become aware of them. Maama Sarah was also living and working within King's College Budo. When faced with my sister's rejection, my mother's friendship with and trust in Maama Sarah became pivotal. She believed deeply in her friend's ability to provide the guidance and discipline I needed to thrive.

Without hesitation and in an era before mobile phones, we got back into the car and drove to Maama Sarah's house to ask if she would kindly take me in. Her home was situated near the boarding girls' quarters on the school grounds, a sharp contrast to my sister's house, which was the first staff house just past the main gate. What could have easily been a moment of defeat turned into an act of faith and quick thinking by my mother. After a short drive, we arrived at our next stop and were met with warm smiles and the welcoming chorus of *Tukutendereza Yesu* repeated again and again—a sound so familiar, so comforting, it felt like a soft landing after a hard fall. My parents, now composed, had clearly decided to discard the earlier incident as the work of the devil trying to steal their joy and frustrate their plans. *Tukutendereza Yesu* echoed once more, filling the air with its reverent melody. I should tell you, *Tukutendereza* is more than a greeting among the *Bazukufu*; it frames every interaction, beginning and ending conversations. Even in the middle of a discussion, if there's a reason to praise God, it will erupt—a testament to their unyielding gratitude.

After the warm greetings, I sat there quietly, watching, and wondering if my parents would share what had transpired earlier. But Maama Sarah, ever discreet, took them aside for a private conversation. They spoke briefly, and in less than an hour, my parents were on their way, leaving me behind to stay and acclimate to the unfamiliar environment. It was the start of a new chapter—one filled with strangeness, uncertainty, and the quiet resolve to adapt to the unknown.

When Maama Sarah walked my parents to the car, I stayed behind. I had already bid them goodbye, knowing I was staying even though I wasn't sure what was next. I felt utterly lost. There was a peculiar restlessness inside me, a sense of being adrift in a world that was too big, too unfamiliar. I had always been curious about everything, but this time, it felt different—like all the new sights, the strange sounds, and the unfamiliar air, were too much to absorb. From the moment the journey from my village had begun to the bustling streets of Kampala, everything had shifted, and I was left standing at the edge of something I literally could not comprehend in my little mind. I walked around the house to find a space to collect myself. Then, I heard the radio. It was soft, almost comforting, coming from an open door. Drawn to it, I wandered into the room, and that's when I saw it.

Opposite the bed, standing tall and strange, was this thing. I couldn't make sense of it at first. A large, reflective surface. I saw... someone who looked exactly like me. It wasn't just a vague resemblance—it was uncanny. I blinked, and they blinked. I waved, and they waved back. Every movement I made, mirrored perfectly.

I stood there, confused and mesmerised. I couldn't understand what I was seeing. I wasn't sure what it was, but it felt familiar, and yet, alien. It wasn't until later that I was told what it was—a mirror. A simple mirror, reflecting the person who stood before it.

It was the first time I truly saw myself in this new world, and it was strange, even surreal. There, in the quiet of that unfamiliar room, with the soft hum of the radio in the background, I was both lost and found. The mirror didn't just show my reflection—it revealed the beginning of a new chapter in my life, one where I would learn to navigate the complexities of who I was becoming in a place so different from everything I had known.

The transition was swift and intense; I had to quickly adapt to an entirely new life. The first challenge was language—Luganda. At the time, I only spoke and understood Runyankore, a language foreign to everyone around me here. Even when they tried, it was difficult to understand each other, as my village accent was thick and unfamiliar. Alongside this, I had to navigate the complexities of learning and speaking English, which was essential to communication in this new world. Maama Sarah quickly introduced me to the Ladybird books, which I was to start reading effective immediately if we were to achieve at least basic communication. Every night, while she worked at her sewing machine, I would sit beside her and read the stories of Peter, Mary, Jane, their dog and their parents in a faraway cottage – the ladybird reading books.

The adjustment wasn't just linguistic. I had to learn unfamiliar social norms, navigate new expectations, and adapt to a pace of life that was utterly different from the communal rhythm I'd known. Every day presented fresh experiences—some confusing, others enlightening—and each one became a quiet teacher. I was discovering not just a new environment, but a new way of being. And the process was anything but easy.

But even in the discomfort, growth was happening.

Through trial, error, and observation, I began to acquire the life skills that would shape my independence: how to cook, clean, be meticulous, care for ducks, and manage responsibilities with care and attention. I was learning resilience, adaptability, and a kind of self-reliance that couldn't be taught in a classroom. These weren't just chores—they were lessons in how to hold myself together in unfamiliar territory.

This chapter of my life began when I was around seven years old, and it would stretch until I turned thirteen, the year I completed primary school. During those formative years, I was planted in unfamiliar soil, but slowly, roots took hold. The world I had entered was new, often overwhelming—but day by day, it became the proving ground where I began to take shape.

Maama Sarah was nothing short of formidable. With a heart full of compassion and a will that could not be swayed, she embodied a rare blend of tenderness and tenacity. Her face bore the calm resolve of someone who had weathered many storms, and her backbone was forged in quiet, unwavering conviction. You couldn't manipulate her. You couldn't buy her. She lived by principle, and her integrity was the kind you could stake your life on. Not just the integrity of her words—but the constancy of her actions, the unshakable consistency of her example.

She took me in with open arms and loved me as though I were her own. She shielded me fiercely, taught me deeply, and extended to me the kind of grace that leaves a permanent mark. And above all, she loved God her whole life—not just in speech, but in posture, discipline, and deed.

While raising her six children—Barbra, Timothy, Winnie, Stephen, Deborah, and Loy—Maama Sarah somehow managed to be everywhere at once. At King's College Budo, she wore many hats: boarding girls' matron, senior lady, headmaster's secretary, and even school tailor, stitching uniform skirts in the evenings when most others had turned in for the day.

But that wasn't all. She farmed too—growing yams, cassava, beans, and bananas in gardens she tended with both faith and grit. Most of the produce fed the family, but sometimes she sold it to the school to stretch her modest salary just a little further. Her resilience wasn't loud—but it was relentless. Resourcefulness and prayer were her weapons; her hands worked the soil, while her knees wore grooves of intercession.

The same rhythm of devotion I had known at home lived here too—daily prayer altars, morning fellowship, evening hymns. Same spirit, different setting. Same God, but a new chapter. Maama Sarah's home carried the discipline of faith and the warmth of love in equal measure—and it became one of the safest places I had ever known.

I vividly recall her typing in her office, a sight that always captivated me when I came back from school. I would pass by her office before heading home, where she had often asked the kitchen staff—Uncle Sam and later James—to save me some food. After eating, I would sometimes wait for her instructions on what was planned for dinner before heading home. Her fingers danced effortlessly across the typewriter keys, and those moments remain etched in my memory. Equally memorable were the late nights when she tirelessly measured, cut, and stitched uniforms. The start of every school year was especially busy, with girls lining up in the compound and on the balcony to try on their skirts, chatting as they waited. Those who hoped for shorter skirts were always disappointed; Maama Sarah had no tolerance for what she deemed "indecent dressing," insisting on proper standards.

Her life was a testament to balance—the rare harmony of tenderness and tenacity. She taught me lessons that continue to guide my life, often quoting scripture such as, "Be ye therefore wise as serpents, and harmless as doves" (Matthew 10:16, KJV). She didn't share it as a lofty ideal but as practical wisdom, showing me that kindness and discernment are not opposites but complements—essential tools for navigating life. Her lessons were never confined to words; they were deeply embedded in her actions, quietly shaping not just my behaviour, but my very soul.

Life with Maama Sarah was a mosaic of rich experiences, each piece intricately placed, creating a vibrant and meaningful whole. The many lively moments left their mark on my soul. Saturdays were usually spent in the faraway gardens where we would weed and harvest crops to sustain us for the week ahead. On weekdays, it was school, work, and tending to the closer garden if a free evening allowed it. Amid the rhythm of hard work, our home stood as a hub of warmth and activity, a place where memories were baked into the very walls—cookies and scones on rainy afternoons, the sparkle of Christmas parties, the joy of end-of-year dinners, and the vibrant hum of boarding house events.

There are no words, no number of lifetimes, that could fully contain who Maama Sarah was to me. She wasn't just present—she was foundational. Everything I am today carries the imprint of her hands and her unshakable way of being. She settled storms and taught me how to carry myself in a world that didn't always make room.

She faced life—head-on, sleeves rolled, heart steady. She made space for others without ever shrinking herself. I saw how she stitched dignity into ordinary days—how nothing was beneath her, and no one above. Because of her, I learned that work is a gift, and that resourcefulness isn't just a skill—it's a mindset. She showed me how to make things last, how to carry grace under pressure, and how to stand tall even when the ground beneath you shifts.

People speak of nature and nurture as though they sit on opposite ends of a scale. I had both. Whatever was born in me—curiosity, resilience, a stubborn streak—was refined under her quiet, persistent watch. The things people now call strengths—my independence, my drive, my ability to adapt and rise—weren't traits I read about. They were etched into me daily by a woman who lived with great purpose long before anyone taught me the word.

I've since walked through fire and favour, but her voice—firm, calm, and always sure—still lives in my choices. If I carry myself with any steadiness today, it's because she carried me first. If I can offer even a flicker of her discernment, her wit, her grounded way of being to my children, I will have done something right. Because she wasn't just in my story. She was the scaffold. The rhythm. The unspoken inheritance.

PART II:

BECOMING

THE HILL THAT RAISED US
A world within Budo and Monica

Living in the vibrant, tightly knit community of King's College was a life unlike any other I had imagined or experienced before. It was a world of its own. The girls from the three dormitories—Gaster, Grace, and Sabaganzi frequently visited the matron's home, which felt like a second sanctuary. It became the go-to place for anything that happened on the girls' side of the school. News reached there first, connecting our lives with theirs in ways that were both practical and, at times, quietly mischievous.

The boarding girls, brimming with youthful energy and mischief, were a constant source of both wonder and amusement. Occasionally, they'd smuggle in their carefully chosen outfits—chic, daring, and usually skimpy—meant for the much-anticipated mixed-house socials with the boys. These "party clothes," as they called them, were wrapped tightly in polythene bags and hidden among the crops in our nearby garden.

On the eve of a party, they'd quietly return, hoping to retrieve their secret stashes. Sometimes they were lucky. Other times, we'd stumble upon the buried bundles while working in the soil. Maama Sarah, ever the vigilant matron, would collect the items and keep them safely locked away. But who dared go ask her for them? No one. And so, during evening roll call, she would announce with calm authority, "Whoever hid their clothes in the garden can come see me at the end of the term." No names. No fuss. Just a quiet, resolute reminder of the discipline and respect she commanded.

Beyond these playful moments, life at King's College was a mix of formal and informal events through which I experienced the world with my developing mind. There were tennis tournaments and spirited inter-house competitions in drama and athletics. I'd eagerly pick a house to support, cheering as if I were one of their own. Founders' Day brought glamour and ceremony as distinguished alumni—many of them national figures—returned to inspire the current students with their stories. Fridays and Sundays were marked by fellowship gatherings, while the sports grounds opposite our home were alive with the thud of basketballs, the crack of cricket bats, and the rhythm of hockey sticks on turf. I soaked it all in, my young heart beating in sync with the life of the school.

But not every moment sparkled. Some days were heavy. On what we called Pavilion Days when a thief was caught on campus, the school police delivered swift and harsh punishment. Watching from a distance, I felt a chill I couldn't quite name—an early lesson in justice, or perhaps the darker side of community order and the realities of life outside our youthful cocoon.

Visiting the sick bay, whether for myself or to check on friends I cared about, became another routine part of my life—a quiet reflection of the vulnerability we all shared in that place.

I can't tell this part of my story without remembering how vividly the world outside King's College Budo echoed within its gates—how history itself threaded its way into our everyday lives.

Even though I wasn't a student enrolled in its classrooms, I lived and breathed the school's rhythm. In fact, I often felt I enjoyed a wider view, untethered by the structure of timetables and uniforms. I was present for everything that mattered. A Budonian in every sense, but freer—watching, listening, absorbing.

I still remember the solemn awe—no, *pride*—that swept through the community in 1993 during the coronation of His Majesty Ronald Muwenda Mutebi II, the Kabaka of Buganda. But it wasn't just pride. It was something deeper. *Majestic pride. Ancestral pride.* The kind that rises quietly from your bones and anchors you to something bigger than yourself.

Though the coronation unfolded beyond the immediate grounds, its presence was everywhere—like a drumbeat rising from the soil, steady and ancestral. You didn't need to be told it was historic. You could feel it in your chest.

Among the Baganda, the Kabaka isn't just a king. He is loved. Deeply. There's a reverence around him that's hard to explain unless you've grown up in it. He represents more than leadership—he carries identity, ancestry, and the heart of a people. You could see it in the way elders spoke, or didn't speak. In the glint in their eyes. In the way, their voices lowered and steadied when they said his name.

Preparations took centre stage. Everything around us bent toward the day—conversations, routines, even lessons. Traditional ceremonies and stories resurfaced like sacred songs remembered from long ago. The younger children were taught the greetings and royal chants; the older ones were taken on excursions to Naggalabi to learn its significance. Buddo Hill had always been special, but now it pulsed with something sacred.

After all, Naggalabi wasn't far—it sat just next door, sharing the hill with King's College, a school built for royalty. Its history wasn't distant; it lived among us. The land itself whispered it. Kings had walked and been crowned here.

You could feel it in the air—the heaviness of history, but also the lightness of joy. Everywhere you turned, someone was humming a royal tune or fixing their attire just so. Every pathway, every classroom, every kitchen buzzed with talk of the big day.

And across the suburb—once just a quiet slope outside Kampala—there was an awakening. Buddo had never felt more alive, more known, more cherished. People travelled in. Flags waved. Drums beat. Every few steps, you heard it: "A*yi Ssaabasajja awangaale!*" Long live the King!

Even if you didn't fully understand it, you *felt* it. You breathed it in. A chapter was being written—and somehow, you were part of it.

Then came 1994, and with it, the haunting news of the Rwandan genocide. Though I was still young, I understood that something unspeakable had taken place. I saw it in the tense expressions of people around me, the quiet urgency in chapel prayers, and the subdued tones that replaced the usual chatter. The weight of it settled over the hill, heavy and still.

That same year also brought a moment of soaring hope: the inauguration of Nelson Mandela as South Africa's first Black president. It wasn't just a political victory—it felt like a continental awakening. His name was spoken at school assemblies with reverence, like that of a prophet or a saint. Even those of us too young to understand the full weight of apartheid could feel the tide turning. It was hope made flesh.

I first heard of it in a moment that blended the faraway with the familiar. Hon. Sam Kuteesa—who was not only a government minister but also the Member of Parliament for my home constituency, Mawogola in Sembabule—had come to pick up his daughters, Shartsi and Charlotte. The girls were in Sabaganzi House, just metres from our home.

When his car pulled up, the buzz started immediately—not just from dorm to dorm, but through the staff quarters too. It was a community, and in a community, everything travelled quickly: every whisper, every glance, every curious ripple of news. The word spread fast—the girls were going to South Africa, to be at Mandela's inauguration.

That evening, I sat quietly with the news, letting it settle. My thoughts wandered, shaping a world of amazement and wonder.

They're going to South Africa? On a plane? To see Mandela?

The Mandela? How does that even feel—sitting in a seat in the sky, watching clouds from above? And being part of something so big? Would they wave at him? Would they be on TV? Would they remember it forever?

I had never been on a plane. I could barely imagine the inside of one. My only knowledge came from pictures and overheard stories.

But something lit up inside me.

Not just excitement—I've always been curious. If I heard current news affairs, I would run with it. But this was more than that. It was a kind of longing. A quiet pull toward things that were bigger than me. Toward people, places, moments, ideas. News, politics, change. I didn't have the words for it then, but looking back, I think it was something I was born with. I cared. I wanted to know. I wanted to understand the world—and maybe, one day, be part of it. And that night, lying in my bed, I wondered: *What would it be like to be one of those girls? To witness history—not from a radio or a chalkboard—but with your own eyes? Did they even know how lucky they were?*

My mind wandered far, full of questions, full of wonder. That kind of news never left me the same.

And then, in 1997, the world seemed to stand still again. It was a Monday morning, and I was on my way to school when I first heard the news. As I passed by a neighbour's home, a radio broadcast was playing—Princess Diana had died. The moment struck me deeply. I remember crying—sobbing or moaning—all the way to school, talking about it as if I understood so much about the world, as if I had known her personally.

I even asked Maama Sarah if I could go to Ms Mirembe's house—the one with a television—so I could watch the funeral. She agreed, and I did go. I was so sad, especially watching her sons walk solemnly behind the coffin. The grief felt strangely personal.

For days afterwards, radios stayed on longer, newspapers were held tightly, and the sense of loss lingered in the air. She wasn't just royalty; she was the embodiment of compassion in a world that so often seemed starved of it.

These weren't just current events; they were the backdrop against which our lives unfolded. They rippled through our conversations and quietly shaped how we came to understand the world. Yet even as history turned on its hinges, everyday life carried on in all its routine and inconvenience. Water was rationed with near-military precision, and electricity blackouts arrived unannounced, often mid-sentence or mid-supper. But somehow, even the darkness had its light—stories told by candle glow, laughter echoing through corridors, the collective thrill when the lights finally blinked back on.

The 1990s didn't just arrive—they charged in, loud and unmissable, and left behind memories that still cling like red dust to school socks. It was a decade that seemed to demand attention. One moment, we were practising curtsies and singing anthems with full lungs; the next, we were trying to make sense of news no child should have to carry. The headlines weren't just stories—they slipped into assemblies, whispers, and even the dinner table.

Those years didn't unfold like pages in a neat textbook. They arrived like surprise guests—some met with dancing and drums, others with silence and heavy pauses. We lived through them, not as passive observers but as children with front-row seats to history, even if we didn't fully grasp it at the time.

Writing about those years fills me with something more than nostalgia. The richness of a childhood shaped not just by love and survival, but by the convergence of personal and historical tides. Though I never had a desk in one of King's College Budo's classrooms, I learned lessons no textbook could contain. History walked through our gates, and I was wide awake for all of it.

Moving on from primary school, which spanned from 1991 to 1997, it was time to step into the next chapter of my life—secondary school. This meant leaving behind the sheltering arms of my guardian angel, Maama Sarah, and moving away to boarding school. Maama Sarah had done her part. I had completed primary school, made friends, and experienced life in ways I had never imagined. You might wonder why I didn't go to King's College, and the answer is simple: it wasn't meant to be. Over time, I've come to accept that fact and find peace in it. I remember Maama Sarah "benching," as we used to call it, for a spot for me many evenings during the application process. The headmaster, Mr Busulwa, however, seemed to hold the view that children of staff—having grown up within the rhythms of the hill—might benefit more from experiencing life beyond it. Perhaps he felt we were already too immersed, too familiar, to engage with the Budonian journey as outsiders did. In hindsight, it was a blessing in disguise. I had lived that hill inside and out; I had tasted all it had to offer. It was time to set my sights on new horizons.

But before I leave this chapter behind, let me introduce you to my day-one friend from primary school—Monica. She, too, lived in King's College and was the daughter of another staff member. For seven years, I walked to and from school with her almost every day. Monica was my loyal, unwavering friend, and still is to this day. She loved and cared for me immensely, looking out for me, especially during the challenging early days when I struggled to communicate. As I mentioned before, I didn't know Luganda or English, and I struggled to pick up on social cues. She became my number one teacher, the one I felt most comfortable turning to with all my confusion about this new world I was navigating.

I'll never forget probably day one or two, as we walked back from school. I turned to her and asked, "How many clothes do they have and how tall are they?" I had seen all these power lines on our walk, and I was astonished by how high they were. Coming from a village that did not have electricity or phone lines, I couldn't wrap my mind around it. It seemed so surreal and perplexing. I remember her patiently, without judgment, explaining to me that these were power lines, not "hang lines" as I had assumed. To this day, I smile at the memory. It is a gentle reminder of how naïve and wide-eyed I was, a little villager stepping into a world so vastly different from my own.

More than anything, it reminds me of Monica's special gift—she didn't just walk beside me; she provided clarity. With her, the world didn't just unfold—it truly bloomed. We played, told stories, and shared dreams. Monica was always the quiet one—an introvert then and still now, though adulthood has gently helped her come out of her shell. Yet, when I had wild ideas, she never hesitated to join me. I was the mischievous one, always seeking adventure. On our walks home from school, I would spot a compound with a tree heavy with fruit and suggest, "Let's just pass by to see." Mangoes hanging over the fence were far too tempting to ignore. Monica, ever gentle and cautious, would give me that look—half concern, half loyalty—and follow along anyway. It was always my idea, little Missy Mischief, with her steady presence by my side.

It's still hard to put into words how much I owe her. When I first started school, I was a girl fresh from the village—clueless about my ABCs, unable to write my name, and wide-eyed at everything around me. Monica was my gentle guide into this new world. In small, consistent ways that never made me feel behind, she helped me catch up. Little by little, I began to grow into myself, and by the time we reached upper primary, a quiet fire had ignited within me.

Competition came naturally after that, not as pressure but as purpose. Judith soon joined our group, and along with two boys—Eimu and Ntege—we became the unofficial top four, competing all the way to Primary Seven. I made it my mission to outdo them, especially in English and Social Studies, while they excelled in Maths and Science. Monica stood by me through it all—helping me revise, celebrating my wins, and finding clever ways to turn rivalry into a playful strategy. If they defeated me in one paper, I'd promise to help them prepare for the next in exchange for their help in my weaker subjects. It became a game of wits, but also of will. With every small victory, I added another layer to the person I was becoming—independent, driven, and quietly determined.

Monica had this incredible ability to help me turn confusion into understanding. She showed me that even the most unfamiliar things could become familiar if you had the right person by your side. From her, I learned that seeing things differently isn't just about clearer vision; it's about having someone who keeps your gaze steady while the world around you shifts.

TAIBAH
A Taste of Liberty

1997 wrapped up with the results from the Primary Leaving Exams, and the journey to secondary school was upon me—big girl now! After failing to secure a spot at Kings College, Maama Sarah and my mother tried for admission to one of the two prestigious all-girls schools that rivalled Budo: Gayaza High School and Namagunga. But, as with many traditional schools, it wasn't just about merit. With places like these, knowing the right people was half the battle—better still, being an alumna. Unfortunately, my mother had neither the connections nor the alumni ties, and her efforts fell short.

    Almost ready to give in to my father's suggestion of sending me to a secondary school closer to home, she had one last conversation with one of her nephews. That conversation turned out to be a game-changer—he mentioned a new all-girls school that was getting good reviews. Without hesitation, my mother seized the opportunity and secured me a spot there. Before long, the shopping for boarding school necessities was done, and I was headed to senior one at Taibah High. It was my first time in boarding school, and while the excitement bubbled up, I couldn't deny the nerves creeping in. Taibah was a Muslim school, and the student body was a unique blend of backgrounds—students from all walks of life, from simplicity to luxury, all coming together in one place. It was like a cultural exchange program, a mini world of its own. I quickly realised to survive and fit in, I would need to tap into my superpower—saying less at first, observing more and making friends. I worked that magic with the enthusiasm of a seasoned pro.

Growing up under Maama Sarah's roof, modesty was not just encouraged but required, I had never been exposed to the world of adornment in quite the same way. Maama Sarah, like my parents, was a *muzukufu*, and in their home, the outward trappings of "worldliness" were unacceptable. No makeup, no jewellery, no growing long hair, no painted nails, and certainly no short dresses. We dressed modestly, naturally, and simply. So, when I saw girls in my new environment at Taibah accessorising—wearing makeup, sporting jewellery, and senior girls flaunting their long natural hair—it was like stepping into a new world. I couldn't help but feel a thrill as I watched them transform into these polished versions of themselves.

And then, the ultimate revelation—jeans. I still don't quite remember if I bought my first pair or if one of my friends gifted them to me, but that moment of wearing jeans was pure freedom. It felt like stepping into a whole new era of self-expression. The simple act of putting them on was a statement of transformation. It was as if I had crossed a threshold, embracing something new and exciting, something I never could have imagined growing up in a home where modesty was the rule. My school life at Taibah wasn't just an academic journey; it was a cultural awakening and modern in a way that felt fresh and exciting compared to the traditional feel of King's College. I quickly embraced the vibe of the school. There was a delicate balance of discipline and liberty, a mix that felt like freedom with just enough structure. It was here that my love for literature was sparked. I was introduced to 'Great Expectations' by Charles Dickens, and I became captivated by Pip, the young boy who, despite all odds, grows into a gentleman through a series of unexpected events. Pip's journey mirrored the tension I was feeling—the contrast between my past and the new world I was stepping into. But it wasn't just literature that expanded my horizons. I began to learn basic Arabic and started exploring the teachings of Islam, immersing myself in a culture and worldview that was both enlightening and enriching. Saturdays at Taibah had a rhythm all their own. After a week of learning and adjusting to the bustling pace of school life, the weekends offered a chance to catch our breath—and, in my case, teach the younger students how to peel green bananas for lunch. It was a task that rotated among the classes every Saturday, but honestly, from where I'd come from, I was more than prepared for it. I found myself looking at those who struggled with the task, eager to teach them the art of peeling bananas—something I had perfected long before I'd stepped foot in this school. While the senior five and six students sometimes got a weekend off to head home, we, the younger ones, had our weekends packed with little activities and plenty of fun.

Some weekends, we spent our time writing songs and laughing through karaoke sessions that could easily have been mistaken for auditions for 'The Worst Singers in the World.' Celine Dion, Toni Braxton, Boyz II Men, Backstreet Boys, and Savage Garden filled the air with songs we belted out—off-key but full of enthusiasm. On other weekends, we'd have live bands and musicians come in, turning our quiet campus into an impromptu concert hall. Sundays brought a different kind of energy altogether. That was when visiting evangelists would come to deliver sermons that were more than just religious teachings—they were life lessons for a group of adolescents trying to figure out what it meant to grow up.

In the middle of each term, we had Visiting Days (VD), a weekend tradition that was always something to look forward to. Parents would show up, arms full of bags bursting with groceries—milk, crisps, sugar, butter, chocolates, bread, yoghurt, and cereals—like they had come to rescue us from a life of deprivation. If your parents missed VD, well, you could be sure that you'd be the saddest girl around. It was a big deal. The dormitory would buzz with excitement, and the night would be filled with the joy of sharing goodies, with everyone comparing what they had been brought.

Since my parents lived so far away in the village, my brother Patrick took on the role of looking after me during these visits. By then, mobile phones were becoming more common, and I had his number memorised by heart. A week before VD, I'd call the office reception, ask the secretary to call him, and casually remind him of the "essentials" I needed. It became our little ritual: I would ask Patrick for specific things, like the newest milk flavour on the market, "Evergreen," some apples, and those interesting foreign snacks I'd seen other students with but had never tried myself. Every single time, Patrick would show up with exactly what I wanted—and often even more. It made me feel like the luckiest girl in school, knowing he remembered the little things that mattered to me.

My time at Taibah, though filled with wonderful memories, came to an unexpected end. On the first Friday of December 1998, as the third term wrapped up and my first year of secondary school ended, my parents arrived to pick me up. With a quiet sense of finality, they asked me to say goodbye to my friends, gently letting me know that I would not be coming back. The emotions crashed over me like a wave. I thought about the friendships I had built and the life I had grown used to. It was hard to imagine leaving it all behind. I felt a deep sadness mixed with uncertainty about what lay ahead. Would my next school be as exciting? Would it be even better? I had no idea. But one thing I did know for sure was that as long as my mother was in charge of where I went, I wouldn't end up at some village school. There was something so reassuring in her voice, a certainty that calmed my restless heart.

Though my time at Taibah was brief, it left lasting memories. It was there I first tasted the freedom of modernity, where I glimpsed a world beyond the protective shell of my previous life. It wasn't just about the friends, the music, or the apples; it was about self-discovery. It was where I learned that life could be both disciplined and filled with liberty, a delicate balance that I would carry with me like a souvenir I'd never outgrow. Taibah had given me a taste of a world far beyond the one I had known, one where fashion, excitement, and new experiences awaited me at every turn.

MPOMA SCHOOL
Toil for Quality and Success

My parents and I spent the first school holiday weekend in Kampala. It was an opportunity to attend the monthly *Bazukufu* fellowship. The Re-Awakened fellowship convenes every first Sunday of the month in Kawempe, drawing a dedicated community from across the nation. This attendance carried a personal purpose as well. My parents would meet and consult with Maama Sarah about tentative options for my next school. They had heard about the liberties at Taibah and had concluded that after the last term, I would not return. They believed this school was offering me more freedom than what a budding teenager like myself could handle responsibly. The concerns were particularly the weekends away from school. After sharing their concerns with Maama Sarah, they asked for her advice and help to find a school with a stronger Christian ethos. After thoughtful discussion, she suggested Mpoma School, mentioning that it aligned with their preferences and that she'd seen an advertisement for available spots and that she would assist in securing my admission. True to her word, she took the initiative. My parents, assured by her guidance, returned home, leaving me in her care.

A few days later, Maama Sarah and I travelled to Mpoma School before its Christmas break. As we journeyed by taxi, I watched Kampala's vibrant chaos gradually fade into the serene countryside. The city's noise softened, replaced by the hum of open fields. When we finally arrived at the school's gate, we signed the visitors' book and made our way to the administration block. The school grounds were striking. Lush, green expanses stretched out in a manner reminiscent of Kings College, tranquil in the quiet of the holiday season. We were welcomed by the assistant principal, who introduced me to the administrator. After a brief interview, the administrator expressed her admiration for my apparent brilliance, though, I'm unsure what I said to earn such praise. Regardless, I was admitted. They handed us a brochure detailing the school's rules, fee payment instructions, and the opening date for the first term.

As I skimmed the packing list later, it became clear that Mpoma was a bastion of discipline. Hair was to be kept at one inch. Nails? Short and unpolished. Knee-high white socks were mandatory, alongside strict limits on personal clothing—no more than four pieces of non-uniform attire, and no shorts, trousers, makeup, jewellery, or other adornments. It was a stark contrast to the liberties I been getting used to, but perhaps it was exactly what I needed.

The holidays passed swiftly, and soon, it was time for a fresh start at Mpoma School, then an all-girls institution. This would be my home for the next three years of ordinary-level secondary school. Perhaps the administrator's words had been more than a compliment—a prophecy of sorts. I excelled academically, consistently ranking among the top students, though mathematics was my Achilles' heel. My aversion to the subject made engagement challenging, and I often struggled.

Socially, however, I flourished. I became part of a tight-knit group of lively, carefree girls. Together, we embraced the joys and mischiefs of teenage life.

True to its mission, the school worked hard to uphold Christian values. We had an active Scripture Union, regular fellowships, and a routine that ended each prep session with a bell calling us to assembly. There, we thanked God for the day, sang praise and worship songs, prayed for the night, and caught up on school news and announcements.

We sang our hearts out in karaoke sessions, exchanged letters with boys from schools like Rubaga Boys and Jinja College, and eagerly awaited the social dance parties we coordinated with them. Of course, we also faced the occasional punishment, usually tied to failed math tests before the revelry of party days. Those were golden times. Sunday evenings were spent catching up to watch Sunset Beach on the common room TV, laughter echoing through the dorms and bonds formed over shared meals, dreams, and adolescent adventures.

I remember when interactions with boys' schools began, assembly time became much more exciting. It was no longer just a routine—it was the moment the entertainment prefect read out the names of mail recipients. If you didn't get a letter, yet we knew a boy fancied you, we'd launch our own "investigation" to figure out what happened. Had he written to someone else? Was it a love triangle? A secret admirer mix-up? Teenage girls, we were part-time detectives, full-time romantics—with a PhD in overthinking and a minor in outrageous gossip. We could cook up conspiracies quicker than a packet of instant noodles!

In the three years I spent there, I was elected dormitory captain twice—what we called the "dormitory mother." This role came with many responsibilities: I looked after the new students assigned to our house, made sure the dorm stayed clean, and enforced lights off and bedtimes. I was also in charge of locking up for class, unlocking for breaks, and ensuring students were accounted for. During the weekends, when teacher supervision was light, I had to mark roll calls and keep an eye on the dorm to avoid the risk of "French leaves" (students sneaking off). I always had to know where my housemates were, in case I had to report their whereabouts. But honestly, the thing that mattered most to me was winning the bed-making competition. This was a big deal! The senior lady and the teacher on duty would judge the competition, and every dorm had to compete. I've always had a bit of a winning streak, so this was something I took very seriously. Even now, making a bed is one of my proudest skills!

Now, speaking of that drive to come out on top—I was a very active member, and at times the leader, of the drama and creative team, and we won a lot of competitions. One year, during the inter-house competitions, my friend Milly and I wrote, directed, and pulled together our own drama show on behalf of our dorm. It was guided by our house leader, who also happened to be the music and French teacher. We won! The prize? A goat! We couldn't wait for roast day to come around, and when it did, it was a real treat—one that sparked envy from the other houses, since there had been no bigger prize to be won than the goat.

Looking back, Mpoma wasn't just a school; it was the place where my strength, brilliance, and the joy of true connection were refined. Many of my friendships born there have endured, standing as a testament to the transformative power of those years.

PATRICK, MY BROTHERMAN

With my parents living so far away in the village, Patrick took on the responsibility of visiting me regularly, always bringing snacks and pocket money. When I was in Senior Three and Four, he worked with Pepsi in sales and distribution, and my school happened to be on his weekly route. He'd often stop by to check on me briefly, and if it was during class, he'd leave an envelope with some cash at the bursar's office.

Patrick was a man I loved, respected, and feared all at once—a mix that all my friends then and now know about. He had this deep, booming voice that could stop you in your tracks. It wasn't so much what he said, but his voice—the authority it commanded—that made me feel a little scared. Even in the light-hearted moments, that feeling lingered. Was it him or the soldier in him? Oh well, let's just say me and my soldier brothers…

I didn't get to know him well until I was about 13. That's when we had our first one-on-one conversation during his visit to Maama Sarah's home. Later, during my Primary Seven vacation, I spent more time with him, and that's when I truly entered his world.

From what I came to learn, Patrick had been a soldier during Museveni's guerilla war, joining as one of the young recruits. At the time, he had just begun A' Level, but left school to join the struggle.

After the war, he was among a select group sent to Libya where—according to what I heard—Gaddafi's army trained them as pilots. He spent several years there. That, I suppose, is why I hadn't known him during my early childhood—he had left before I was old enough to form lasting memories.

When he eventually returned home, many of his peers had resumed their education, risen through the ranks, married, and were well into the next chapters of their lives. That realisation, I was told, led him to make a bold decision: to leave the army and return to school—starting, quite incredibly, with high school, the very level he had left behind years earlier.

Over time, the more I got to know him and his story, the more I admired him—a great deal.

During the time I spent with him, I began to see him in a new light. He was thoughtful, caring, and so much more than I had imagined. He spoiled me in the best ways, showering me with a kind of tenderness that left a mark on my memories. Because of him, I quietly set the bar high for the kind of man I wanted in my life—someone like my father or at least like Patrick.

What I didn't realise back then, but came to understand later, was how romantic he really was. I discovered this side of him not through our talks, but by sneaking peeks at his diaries. I know, that sounds intrusive, and yes, I told him years later that I had read them. As I flipped through those pages, I was amazed at how openly he poured out his heart. I remember thinking, "Wow, my brother is so romantic." It wasn't the cliché stuff; it was deeper, more genuine. He wrote with a sensitivity I had never encountered before, capturing every little feeling, every ache and dream, like he was trying to hold onto those moments forever.

He was also incredibly clever. He had this knack for detail, always working on crossword puzzles and leaving clippings behind—each filled in with care. It showed how much he loved a challenge and wasn't afraid of complexity.

Patrick shared his place with his housemate, Wilson, who treated me like the little sister they both never had. Being around them felt like being wrapped in a warm blanket of love—one that asked for nothing in return but gave so freely. Looking back, it all makes sense why I thought so highly of Patrick. He wasn't perfect, but he was always there, thoughtful, and quietly extraordinary in so many ways that I'm still uncovering.

THE END OF ONE STAIR, THE START OF ANOTHER
Namirembe Hillside High School

The three meaningful years I spent at Mpoma came to a bittersweet end when I finished Senior Four. After that came the usual short break—a few months of rest while we waited for our results and prepared for A' Level. It was a welcome pause, filled with some well-earned relaxation and a bit of wandering before I moved on to another school for my next chapter.

By this time, private schools were springing up like wildflowers, creating a bustling and competitive environment. It felt like everyone was on edge, eager to prove themselves. Schools were no longer just about good grades; they were judged by how many students they could send off with government sponsorship. You could feel the tension and ambition in the air, with each school vying for recognition and striving to be the best—not just for themselves but for the families and communities they represented. In this world, the pursuit of success was deeply personal, linking dreams and aspirations to every student's journey.

My mother always took education seriously, as you know by now. During my vacation, she started speaking with friends and relatives to find out which school was currently the best performing. In contrast, my father had a more cautious viewpoint. He frequently reminded me that if I didn't do well, Senior Four could mark the end of my education.

"I don't have any cows left to sell for your school fees," he would say. "The coffee doesn't bring in much anymore, and my health isn't good enough to tend to it. Your mother encouraged me to send you to these private schools in Kampala, but if your results are poor, there's no point in wasting money we don't have. You might as well get married instead."

Sometimes he'd point out other girls my age, saying, "Look at so-and-so's daughter—she got married when her parents couldn't afford to send her for higher education, and she's doing just fine." He'd also reminisce about how much more affordable education had been in my older siblings' time. Back then, missionary schools provided free education for students who excelled academically and came from humble backgrounds. He'd tell me stories of how my older siblings benefited from such opportunities, but times had changed, and those options no longer existed.

At the time, my father was already in his 70s, and decades of hard, physical work—tending the coffee farm and supporting the family—had taken a serious toll on his health. His mobility was getting more and more restricted, and he battled persistent heart problems and osteoarthritis. During my vacation, he spent most of his time in Kampala at David's home, where he could receive proper medical care and consult with doctors.

His absence at home only deepened my anxiety. Even though he wasn't there, his words seemed to linger everywhere—like echoes bouncing around my mind every single day. I understood how crucial my results would be; they weren't just numbers on a page but had the power to shape my entire future. If I performed well enough to move forward, I'd need to invest everything I had into the next two years of higher education. It felt like my whole life balanced on this one moment.

While the specifics of that time are hazy, one thing stands out: there was a constant undercurrent of worry in our house. I unexpectedly found myself stepping into the role of the adult, which felt overwhelming. The weight of responsibility pressed heavily on my shoulders as each day passed, creating a tangled mix of anticipation and uncertainty—not only about my results but also about my father's health.

Then, the moment I'd been anxiously waiting for finally arrived: the results. I had passed. At the same time, my father came home looking healthier than he had in a long time. Good news has a way of coming just when you need it most, and for a little while, everything felt lighter. I could finally breathe again.

In the days that followed, I focused on preparing for what was next. I travelled to Kampala and stayed for a while with Patrick and his wife, Catherine, in their flat on Buganda Road. The steady rhythm of their lives provided me with the respite I needed.

Amidst the whirlwind of preparation and transition, there was still space for a little rebellion. With encouragement from my friends, and the quiet support of Justine, Patrick and Catherine's housekeeper (whom I'd beg to cover for me if Pat returned and I wasn't home), I managed to sneak away from their home to meet up with friends. We'd gather at Blitz Video for ice cream, the Lebanese restaurant for a cheap lunch or snack, or indulge in Chipper Adams' ice cream. And of course, there was Fido Dido, the rooftop venue on Kampala Road, and Striker's Room, where the trans-day dance parties brought together vacationists like me from all over—especially those of us who had been in single-sex schools, all girls or all boys. It was exciting to mingle and socialise in a way we hadn't before. Those afternoons, filled with music, laughter, and the buzz of new connections, were a welcome escape from the weight of the near future. They offered a brief, intoxicating taste of freedom, untouched by the pressures of what A' level would bring. I lived it up, convincing myself it was a well-earned celebration—I had made it this far... or so I thought.

Soon, the carefree days came to an end, and it was time to face the next chapter: advanced-level education—a season that felt like an unspoken call to grow up. My mother, ever determined about my education, chose to send me to one of the most prestigious private A' level schools, despite its hefty price tag. Her hope was that I'd achieve the grades necessary to secure a coveted government sponsorship for university.

Namirembe Hillside High School was like Taibah on steroids—a vibrant melting pot of students from every corner of the nation. Each brought their own unique backgrounds, family dynamics, and, most strikingly, a wide array of social classes. This diversity wasn't just visible; it was tangible, shaping every interaction and experience. For me, it was a whole new world to navigate, far beyond my imagination of what A' level would be. It was a mixed school with boys—a stark contrast to the all-girls environments of Taibah and Mpoma I had grown accustomed to. The shift was both exhilarating and daunting, pushing me to adjust to a rhythm that was unfamiliar yet thrilling in its novelty.

The school was teeming with students of varying heights, skin tones and body builds. Everywhere I turned, there were so many of them, each seemingly caught up in their own individual journey, yet somehow intertwined in the same grand narrative of the same story. At first, it felt overwhelming, the sheer magnitude of it all. Yet, amidst the chaos, something was fascinating too, being surrounded by such a mix of humanity, a kaleidoscope of lives, experiences and stories waiting to be shared and explored.

The school had excelled in the previous HSC results, earning nationwide recognition through newspaper headlines. Many of its students earned government sponsorships at various universities, a moment of immense pride for the founders and everyone connected to the school. This success sparked a surge of interest from parents, resulting in our intake that year being the largest the school had ever seen. In fact, our class was so large that we couldn't all be accommodated at the same time, leading to two separate intakes within the same year. We had classes in shifts because there wasn't a classroom large enough to fit all the students offering similar subject combinations at once. In response, a makeshift wooden classroom was hastily constructed, and we cheekily named it 'Timberland. It was a space unlike any traditional classroom—dusty, chaotic, and perpetually bustling with noise. Picture a lively marketplace, but instead of merchants and goods, there were students in uniform, clutching books and pens. The teachers faced an uphill battle, struggling to maintain order amidst the constant flurry of activity. Conversations buzzed in the corners, papers rustled incessantly, and the occasional burst of laughter would ripple through the room like an uninvited guest. Often, the back of the classroom felt like a world of its own, far removed from the teacher's line of sight. Despite the challenges, "Timberland" became its own kind of ecosystem, where chaos and learning somehow coexisted, each vying for dominance in the dusty wooden arena.

It didn't take long for me to adjust to the whirlwind that was Namirembe Hillside. Slowly, I found my footing in this sea of unfamiliar faces and carved out a space for myself within the vast, diverse group. I managed to make friends, mostly those who shared my love for literature. Our bond was cemented by shared laughter at Kyali's jokes in class, his dark sense of humour providing a strange yet endearing levity, and Hillary's paradoxical blend of seriousness and light-hearted storytelling during his divinity lessons.

Just as I was settling in, the second intake returned from their short break—a logistical shuffle to accommodate our record-breaking class size. It was during this time that Ambrose asked me out. His quiet, unassuming demeanour had already piqued the interest of several girls, I later learned. There was something about him—calm, self-contained, and wise beyond his years. He carried himself with a maturity that seemed almost out of place among teenagers, coupled with a gentlemanly charm that made him stand out even more.

Ambrose's reserved nature had kept him from mingling much with the first cohort, only heightening his mystique. So, when he expressed interest in me—a girl who had only just arrived, dressed without any flair or the polish I had seen in others—it sparked a wave of envious stares and whispered gossip. This was my first relationship, and for me, it was a significant moment. Coming from a background so different from the one I now found myself in, it felt surreal to have captured the attention of someone like him. It wasn't just about the relationship itself; it was a quiet affirmation that I could find my place in this new, intimidating world.

Life at this school unfolded in a series of unforgettable episodes— each one more vivid, layered, and full of character than the last. The days moved to the rhythm of routine and surprise, shaped by a cast of teachers who were systematic, often disciplinarian, and occasionally, delightfully dramatic.

Literature was with the ever-passionate Mr Kyali, whose voice could thunder or whisper—depending on whether we were tackling the grim solitude of *Darkness at Noon*, the tension between

Rubashov's conscience and ideology, the fiery wit between Darcy and Elizabeth Bennet, or the tragic unravelling of *Othello*.

Divinity was with Hillary, and it felt less like a subject and more like theology—a deep dive into a version of the Bible we had never quite seen before, full of layers and revelations we didn't know to expect.

Economics was with the meticulous Naboth, who somehow turned supply-and-demand graphs into moral debates, making us question more than just markets and curves.

Beyond the classroom, life unfolded in Technicolor. *Timberland*—the fabled ground zero of all our youthful mischief, dreams, discoveries, and secret rendezvous—was where boundaries were tested, friendships forged, and hearts, sometimes, broken and mended again. Each of us knew its corners, its echoes, its stories. It was less a place and more a rite of passage.

Then came the canteen hours—almost sacred, certainly non-negotiable. No matter how pressing the day's demands, we would show up without fail, pulled like magnets by the rich aromas that floated through the air. Getting in often required a strategic push or two (and maybe a nudge from a hungry elbow), but the effort was always worth it. The food—simple, familiar, utterly delicious—was more than sustenance; it was a gathering, a ritual, a joy.

But as the saying goes, time flies—not just when you're having fun, but when the slow and steady wheels of transformation are quietly turning beneath you. In what felt like a blink, the two years of A' Level passed, carrying away with them the final wisps of childhood innocence and the protective comfort of structured boarding life. Suddenly, the cocoon of school and home gave way to something unfamiliar. I stood at the edge of a threshold—where everything I knew seemed to fall behind, and everything ahead was yet unknown.

It was a strange in-between time. The long holiday began in early November and stretched into the following year, offering a deceptive calm before the results would arrive. Those results held the power to define what came next: If the hard work, long nights, and prayers of the past two years bore fruit, I would go on to university, to chase bigger dreams. If not, I would be thrust into the open world, not entirely prepared but determined to walk forward anyway—with faith, grit, and whatever lessons life had already tucked beneath my skin.

A DISCIPLINE OF BECOMING

The world had cracked open before me—an invitation and a challenge—and time, almost ceremoniously, had laid out a new table. On it was a metaphorical shopping bag, handed to me by life itself, full of possibilities, decisions, and the weight of personal responsibility. It felt as though I had been dropped into a vast, unfamiliar mall—life's sprawling marketplace—without a shopping list. And as with all malls, the danger wasn't in what wasn't there; it was in being overwhelmed by everything that was. Without clarity, you could walk out carrying things that only looked good but served no real purpose—or worse, walk out empty-handed, paralysed by indecision. Both outcomes carried lasting consequences. I came to understand that I had to be intentional, deliberate, and even about the choices I made. But clarity did not come easily. Decisions, I realised, were a muscle I had to train. Mistakes were inevitable, and I braced myself to make them. After all, how else would I learn that fire burns unless I touched it?

What mattered most to me at the time was finding a holiday job. I was determined—unyielding, even—about securing one, regardless of how steep the odds were. I couldn't bear the thought of lounging around the village in the comfort of home while time ticked on without a plan. Whether my exam results turned out well or not, I knew I needed to take the next step.

Plan A was clear: pass well and earn a government-sponsored spot at Makerere University. Plan B? Find work and begin planting seeds for a future in that direction. Either path was valid, but both demanded courage. What made the journey more daunting was the reality I had come to accept—I wasn't anyone's child of influence. Yes, I had relatives in prominent positions, including a general for a brother, but leaning on their names or connections wasn't something I was willing to do. I was more afraid of burning bridges than I was of building from scratch.

I was resolute in my decision to carve my own path—with God's help. I knew who I was and the values I stood for, and I wanted every step forward to honour that foundation. My friends were in the same phase of limbo—young, ambitious, filled with dreams, and yet uncertain about the roads that lay ahead. We were all grasping for something solid, learning to navigate transition without a map. But I had faith that the next step would reveal itself if I continued to walk forward with courage.

Up until this point, giving up had never once found room in my life's story, and I couldn't afford to introduce it now—not when the stakes felt higher than ever. The risks were real. The odds were stacked. However, I believed that persistence was still the most powerful leverage I had.

So, I took my time. I researched. I prayed. I combed through potential places where I might work—places that not only aligned with my values, but that wouldn't draw frowns or concern from my parents. That intentional search led me to New Day Bookshop—a place that would later rebrand as FreshVine.

Fuelled by quiet determination, I began frequenting the bookshop day after day asking if they had a job available. I didn't just inquire; I offered to help in any way I could. Whether it meant sweeping the floors, dusting the shelves or unpacking deliveries. I made it clear I was ready to work, even without pay. I was willing to volunteer just to have a foot in the door.

Each time, the owner kindly explained they didn't have any vacancies. She was always gracious, never dismissive, and that made it easier to keep returning even when I left empty-handed. Still, I refused to give up. Something in me knew that consistency had its own voice—that eventually, showing up would say something that words couldn't.

FRESHVINE BOOKSHOP

After about a month of knocking on that same door, my persistence finally bore fruit.

Charity, whom we affectionately called Auntie Charity, told me they didn't have any specific role for me but that my persistence as a young person had left quite an impression. She said she believed God had sent me her way—and that alone made her want to understand who I was and where I came from.

As I shared more about my parents, she didn't recognise them personally, but she lit up at the mention of some of my siblings. Their names and stories seemed to stir familiarity, and in that moment, a deeper connection was formed.

Inspired by something beyond logic—perhaps faith, perhaps motherly instinct, she took me by the hand and led me upstairs to the office of James, the bookshop's accountant. With warmth and a hint of pride, she introduced me as "the young, persistent girl who had made it her mission to come by asking for a job." Then, looking at James with resolve, she said, "Find a way she can be of use in this store."

That's how my new day dawned—or rather, how opportunity flung its door wide open to a ready, willing, and desperate recipient.

This wasn't just any job. It was at a Christian bookshop—a place of purpose, peace, and alignment with everything my parents believed in. I knew they would not only approve but rejoice, seeing this as a door opened by God Himself. And there was more: the owner wasn't just any businesswoman. She was the accomplished, born-again daughter of one of Uganda's most revered Christian leaders—Bishop Festo Kivengere.

Bishop Festo's legacy stood tall and clear in the hearts of believers across Uganda and beyond. He was often referred to as the "Billy Graham of Africa," a man who travelled the world proclaiming the gospel with a fire that never dimmed. His name wasn't just respected—it was revered. He had been a bold voice of truth in one of Uganda's darkest chapters, courageously speaking out against the brutal regime of Idi Amin.

After the assassination of Archbishop Janani Luwum in 1977, Bishop Festo fled into exile for his safety. Yet even from afar, his voice remained loud and steady. It was in that season he wrote the profound book I Love Idi Amin—not as a passive slogan, but as a radical testimony of forgiveness. In it, he confronted pain with grace, hatred with love, and tyranny with the transforming power of Christ. His life wasn't just a message, it was a movement of faith, courage, and divine reconciliation.

So yes, this job meant so much more than a paycheck or experience. It connected me in a way to a spiritual heritage rooted in conviction and courage.

Back at the bookshop, I was introduced to a range of responsibilities that would soon become second nature. I was taught how to do stock-taking, replenish shelves, code and price items, communicate with suppliers, and handle any other task assigned to me with diligence. It wasn't glamorous work, but it was meaningful, and I was learning fast. I was trusted, and that trust gave me a sense of belonging.

With the job secured, however, a new challenge quickly emerged: finding a place to stay. The opportunity had opened, yes—but it hadn't come with room and board. I now had to figure out not just how to work, but how to live near enough to keep showing up on time and ready. It was the next stretch of faith and the next test of persistence.

My cousin Rose, one of the two older daughters of my Uncle Nguna, lived just a stone's throw from the bookshop—no more than a one-minute walk. On the surface, it seemed perfect. A safe, familiar home within reach of my new job. So, I asked my father if he would speak to her on my behalf and request that she allow me to stay with her. It wasn't that I couldn't speak for myself, but I didn't have any real relationship with Rose beyond being family. My father, on the other hand, wasn't just her uncle—he had played a significant role in raising her. I felt he was the best person to make such a request with both grace and familiarity.

He did. He spoke to her. But she took time to respond—too much time. And time, for me, was no longer a luxury. The job was secured, yes, but the clock was ticking. I needed a place to stay if I was going to hold onto the opportunity I'd worked so hard to get.

So, I decided to follow up myself.

On a bright Saturday afternoon, I visited Rose. After some pleasantries and small talk, I brought up the request gently, hoping for a warm reply. Instead, I was met with a polite but indirect decline. She didn't say no outright, but her words said enough. I understood. The door was closed. The refusal hit hard. Not just because of the inconvenience, but because of what it reminded me of. It echoed Mary's response when my parents asked her for help when I was only seven. It triggered a familiar ache: that sharp, childlike confusion when help is withheld without explanation.

Why were people like this?

I was just a child then. And even now, as a young adult trying to build a life with integrity, I was still met with the same wall of rejection. But this time, it didn't sting in the same way. Maybe it was because I was older. Maybe it was because I had learned, however painfully, that no one owes you anything in this life.

Still, the reasons behind that kind of quiet meanness—the subtle coldness masked in politeness continued to elude me. It was a wound that didn't bleed but lingered. A shadow that didn't consume me but followed. For many years, I carried it quietly.

But that's a story for another time.

DESTINY HELPER

After that disappointment, I reached out to a dear friend, Phiona. She was someone I trusted deeply and whose consistency had always been a source of comfort. At the time, she was a law student living in a modest one-bedroom apartment near her university in Kansanga. It was quite a distance from the bookshop in Kampala, but I didn't hesitate. I was confident she wouldn't mind having me stay with her. And thankfully, I was right. Without a second thought, Phiona welcomed me into her space with warmth and generosity.

Phiona and I had met back in Mpoma, though she had been at the A' level at the time while I was still at the O' level. Despite the age and difference in our academic years, we shared a rare and lasting bond. I had served as dormitory mother, and Phiona was chief justice of the student council—a role that spoke to her natural authority, fairness, and unwavering sense of justice. We were both leaders in different ways, and our paths often crossed not just in duty, but in shared values and quiet mutual admiration.

It's no wonder she's now an esteemed magistrate. The seeds of leadership, empathy, and clear judgment were already evident back then.

Staying with her gave me more than just a roof over my head, it gave me a small island of familiarity in a sea of newness and uncertainty.

Her apartment wasn't big, but it was peaceful. It carried the scent of warm meals, law books, and late-night studying. The rhythm of her disciplined life grounded me. I now had somewhere to return to after work. A place where I could exhale, reflect, and regroup.

The commute from Kansanga to the city was long and tiring, and it demanded early mornings and late returns. Still, I considered it a small price to pay. Every day, I woke up determined not to waste the opportunity I had been given. I was no longer waiting for life to happen to me—I was in it, actively navigating the twists, uncertainties, and hidden graces of adulthood.

So, with a place to stay finally secured, I dove headfirst into this big, unpredictable world—no guarantees, no shortcuts. I was loudly aware that my survival, my success, or my failure would depend entirely on the choices I made from that point forward.

At FreshVine, I gained invaluable skills and practical tools essential for running a small bookshop enterprise. I learned how to manage stock, organise shelves, handle customer service, and contribute meaningfully to a place that was more than just a store. But beyond the technical know-how, the job offered something far more lasting: spiritual nourishment.

Each morning at 8 a.m., before the shop doors opened, Auntie Charity led us in devotions. These sessions weren't just routine, they were sacred. They grounded us in faith, reminded us why we were there, and set a tone of purpose for the entire day. In those quiet moments of shared scripture and prayer, I found deep encouragement, fresh perspective, and the strength to carry myself with grace and gratitude, even when the day ahead was uncertain or demanding.

The relationships I formed during this time were incredibly meaningful. My colleagues—James, Francis, Sam, Esther, and later Fred and David, who is Auntie Charity's nephew—were kind, helpful, and dedicated. Many of our customers were fellow Christians, including ministers, students, teachers, and believers seeking truth, knowledge, or just a peaceful place to browse. These daily interactions became little windows of connection and light. Each encounter contributed something to my life—whether it was wisdom, patience, joy, or a simple reminder of the importance of kindness.

Being the only one among my close friends who had a job at that time gave me a quiet, deep sense of pride. I wasn't boastful, but I was grateful. Whenever they were in the city, they would stop by for a quick catch-up, laughs, updates, and encouragement. I cherished those moments. They reminded me how far I'd come. I was carving out a path, one I could call mine. And every time one of them walked in, I felt anchored. I was becoming.

Working at FreshVine also allowed me to immerse myself in a world of spiritual literature and gospel music. Day after day, I was surrounded by books that fed my soul—devotionals, biographies, teachings, and testimonies from Christian voices across the world. The atmosphere was always filled with soft gospel music playing in the background, creating a peaceful, worshipful ambience. At times, it felt less like a retail space and more like a quiet sanctuary. It was soothing, grounding and beautiful.

Truthfully, it was in this space that I came to know so many international preachers, evangelists, and musicians—names I had never heard before became part of my daily rhythm. I listened to Joyce Meyer's unfiltered honesty, read Myles Munroe's insights on purpose and leadership, and soaked in T.D. Jake's bold, spirit-stirring messages. I discovered Don Moen, Michael W. Smith, and CeCe Winans—and their music became a soundtrack to those quiet workdays, each song layering faith upon faith.

I encountered the writings and messages of God's Generals and began to appreciate the weight of their legacies—their courage, faith, failures, and the fire that marked their ministries. My world expanded in ways I hadn't expected. I wasn't just learning how to sell Christian content; I was living in it, absorbing it, and slowly being transformed.

It was also at FreshVine that my entrepreneurial spirit began to quietly take shape.

While working there, I noticed an opportunity, one that stirred something inside me. The shop often sourced gifts from various external suppliers: bookmarks, mugs, wall art, keychains, and other Christian keepsakes. I began to wonder: why couldn't I be one of those suppliers?

I envisioned sourcing unique and distinctive gifts from shops across town and supplying them to the bookshop. But I also understood the risk of perceived conflict of interest. So before doing anything, I approached Auntie Charity and openly shared my idea. I told her I didn't want to overstep or create tension. She listened quietly, then, without hesitation, said yes.

Her support gave me confidence, and soon I began visiting suppliers across Kampala, handpicking items that aligned with the shop's values and aesthetic. It started small, but it brought in a bit of extra income—and more importantly, it awakened something in me: resourcefulness, creativity, and the quiet thrill of building something of my own.

That side venture, though modest, taught me lessons that went far beyond profit. It showed me how to spot a gap and fill it. How to balance employment with initiative. How to ask, humbly, and take a risk. It complemented my salary, yes—but more than that, it became a training ground for the years ahead.

Working at FreshVine sustained me spiritually, emotionally, and financially in ways I hadn't anticipated. It was a challenging but rewarding chapter that laid the foundation for creativity, initiative, and resourcefulness—qualities that would guide me in years to come.

FreshVine was more than just a job—it became a sanctuary and a welcome distraction that kept my mind from spiralling into the anxiety of waiting for my results.

The uncertainty of whether I had passed or failed and what that would mean for my future—loomed in the background, but it didn't consume me the way it could have. FreshVine offered me a steady place to stand. There was structure, purpose, and a sense of progress. I wasn't idle. I wasn't stuck. I was doing something that mattered, and that grounded me.

In those days, my greatest fear wasn't just academic failure, but disappointing my parents, especially my mother. She had charted my educational journey with such care and precision, always seeing potential in me, and steering me toward something better. She had sacrificed, prayed and planned. The thought of letting her down was heavier than the fear of any grade on a paper.

And yet, somewhere along the way, something shifted.

I began to believe that even if the results didn't turn out the way we hoped, even if Plan A fell through—I would still have options. I could continue working at FreshVine, maybe enrol in a course, and slowly carve out a different path. One that was still meaningful. One that was still mine. The future no longer felt like impending doom. It felt open. Maybe not easy, but no longer terrifying.

I had found a sense of direction, even before the results came in.

But I couldn't ignore my father's warning—if I didn't achieve the grades required for government sponsorship, he would have no choice but to marry me off. It wasn't a threat delivered in anger, but a sobering reality. He had already sold many cows to support my secondary education, and there was no money left for university fees. That knowledge sat heavily with me. This was precisely why I had been so determined to secure a job before the results came back—I needed a backup plan.

THE MOMENT OF TRUTH

After months of anticipation, the results finally arrived.

The news was overwhelming. Not only had I passed, but I had excelled far beyond my expectations. I was eligible for government sponsorship! It felt surreal. I knew I had worked hard, but even I was stunned by how well I had done. God had heard my prayers and undoubtedly, the faithful prayers of my mother too.

The joy that followed was indescribable. After all the fear, uncertainty, and silent battles, this was a victory wrapped in grace. This was a confirmation that every step, every tear, every sleepless night had not been in vain.

Of course, the news wasn't welcome to everyone. For some—like Mary—my success was an inconvenient truth.

Just before the results came back, Mary learned I was working at FreshVine. She doubted it could be true. Knowing Auntie Charity personally, she couldn't imagine that I had secured a position there without connections or influence. In her mind, opportunities like that weren't earned on merit, certainly not by someone like me. It was easier for her to believe there had been some backdoor arrangement than to accept that persistence and favour had opened the door.

Rather than asking me directly, she chose to twist the story. She told my parents that I was working at Kampala Club, a private, members-only establishment. The implication was clear and damaging. She framed it in a way that cast doubt on my character and intentions.

Her words, laced with just enough concern and disbelief, were enough to unsettle my parents. They didn't question me. They didn't call. They simply decided to verify things for themselves.

One day, while I was in the back of the shop attending to a customer, I noticed Auntie Charity walking toward me with my mother beside her.

The sight froze me. I hadn't been expecting my mother, and for a moment, I couldn't make sense of what was happening. Why was she here? Had something happened? My mother didn't explain right away. She didn't come with accusation or confrontation. Instead, she turned to Auntie Charity and thanked her sincerely and earnestly for everything she had done for me.

She spoke with deep appreciation, saying how rare it was for someone to employ a young girl like me. "Without connections, or being 'so and so's child,'" she said, "who does that these days?" Her gratitude was unmistakable. She had come with questions—perhaps even suspicion—but left with assurance. Whatever doubts had been planted were now gently uprooted and replaced by something stronger: truth, trust, and quiet pride.

And in that moment, I felt both seen and vindicated.

The assumptions, the whispered criticisms, and the quiet suspicions all faded in the face of something far more powerful evidence. I had earned my place. And for the first time in a long while, I saw in my mother's eyes not just relief, but a deep sense of confidence in who I was becoming.

When we were alone, my mother finally told me the real reason for her visit. She admitted that she had come because Mary claimed I wasn't working at FreshVine but at Kampala Club. I was stunned. I had never even heard of Kampala Club.

Curiosity swirled through my mind. What sort of story had Mary told them? What kind of place had she described and what image had she painted of me working there? It was painful to imagine. Her doubts had been sharp enough to shape suspicion in my parents' hearts, pushing them to verify the truth for themselves.

But thankfully, Auntie Charity, in her warmth and honesty, had unknowingly put all those concerns to rest. She had spoken with gratitude about me, never knowing she was defending me. God, as always, had covered me. The truth had surfaced, not because I forced it, but because it simply stood on its own.

My mother left that day reassured. And I was left even more grateful—not just for the job at FreshVine, but for the deeper lessons it was teaching me. I had learned about integrity, and God's quiet but powerful protection. Looking back, I can't help but think of the words of King David in Psalm 23:5:

"Thou preparest a table before me in the presence of mine enemies: thou anointest my head with oil; my cup runneth over." (KJV)

FreshVine was that table for me. A place of provision, favour, and covering set by God right in the presence of those who doubted or sought to undermine me. It was a sacred space where I was nurtured, protected, and strengthened for the road ahead.

To some, it might have seemed like just a small Christian bookshop. A modest job. An ordinary opportunity.

But to me, it was everything.

It gave me the chance to shape a future at a time when everything else felt fragile and uncertain. It wasn't about the wage—I wasn't working just to get by. I was working to prove something to myself:

that I could rise above my circumstances. That my story wasn't over just because the odds were high. No matter how others perceived me, God had opened a door no one could shut.

My parents beamed with pride, and the news spread quickly through the village: I was going to Makerere University.

In that moment, I couldn't help but think back to the words of the administrator from years ago—words that had once seemed distant and ambitious, now ringing with undeniable truth. Her prophecy had come to life.

Makerere, the most prestigious university in Uganda, has long stood as a symbol of academic excellence and national pride. It is not just a university—it is a legacy. A place that has shaped presidents, scholars, scientists, creatives, and change-makers who have left their mark not only in Uganda but across the world. Its name carries weight. Its graduates carry influence. And now, somehow, I was going to be counted among them.

I felt a mix of awe, excitement, and overwhelming gratitude. This was no small milestone. This was a door few could open, and it had opened for me.

The pride my parents felt was immeasurable. For years, they had poured themselves into me—believing in my potential, even when the path seemed uncertain. They had sacrificed in silence, prayed in faith, and pushed me gently but consistently toward something greater. To them, I had always been their precious child. This achievement wasn't just mine; it was theirs too. A shared victory and dream for me.

At this time, I was still living with my dear friend Phiona, whose family had so graciously embraced me as one of their own. Her home had become a place of refuge and belonging, where I felt seen, safe, and valued. Phiona's mother was known for her warmth. She had a quiet, natural way of making everyone feel welcome.

Whether you were family or friends, her love was the same. She treated her children's friends like her own, and I was no exception. In her presence, I didn't feel like a guest, I felt like a daughter. They had become my family. And in that season, wrapped in the embrace of their kindness and generosity, we created memories that would last a lifetime.

As I began preparing for university, buying the necessary items and gathering the resources for this new chapter, I couldn't help but reflect on the journey that had led me here. So much had happened in such a short time. I had climbed hills I thought I wouldn't, overcome fears I hadn't spoken aloud, and seen God's hand at work in ways I couldn't deny.

During this time, I remember experiencing some tension with Ambrose. I don't recall what caused the strain, but it left an emotional ripple. Despite the occasional disagreements, he remained an important part of my life. We still visited each other whenever we could, holding onto the small but meaningful moments that kept the relationship alive, even with its bumps and uncertainties.

Through it all, God had been taking care of me—quietly, consistently, and sometimes, miraculously.

One morning in particular stands out in my memory. I was standing by the roadside, waiting for a taxi, but I had no transport money. None. I stood there, wondering how I would explain to the conductor that I couldn't pay. My mind spun through possible words and imagined reactions. I was anxious, embarrassed, and uncertain.

And then, out of nowhere, a car pulled over.

Two men, on their way to the city, offered me a lift. I don't remember their names or their faces, only the overwhelming sense that they had been sent. It was as if heaven had whispered to earth on my behalf. On that day, I had no way of getting to work—and yet, God made a way.

It was a moment that reinforced something I had always believed but now felt deeply: God works in mysterious ways. He sees the smallest needs and answers them with care. Even when I have nothing, He ensures I lack nothing. That day, I was reminded again that His provision isn't always loud—but it is always timely.

With a heart full of gratitude, I stepped into this new season. I didn't know what Makerere would hold—what joys, what challenges, what lessons—but I knew one thing for sure: I would not be walking into it alone.

Apologies for the nitty-gritty details—but sometimes, it's those very moments, the quiet and often overlooked ones, that deserve to be highlighted. They may not paint the full picture, but they carry the texture of real life. What an interesting journey it's been so far! Woven with unexpected turns, quiet miracles, and grace that often showed up in small, unannounced ways.

As they say, the days slip away faster than you realise—or maybe that's just how it felt when I was fully engaged in everything around me. Or perhaps it was a bit of both. Either way, the weeks passed quickly, and before I knew it, the next step stood clear: it was time to start preparing for university.

There was an undeniable excitement in the air. It felt as though we had all been in some kind of hibernation, tucked away in caves of waiting and anticipation—just longing for that first breath of sunlight to break through. And now, here it was. The moment we had all been preparing for.

Conversations among friends grew more frequent, more joyful, and full of hope and laughter. We were all buzzing with the same kind of energy—sharing the news, catching up more often, marvelling at the possibilities. It was a moment of connection, a time to pause and celebrate what was ahead.

I remember meeting up with my friend Irene on a beautiful afternoon. We had made plans to visit Makerere University, to check the notice boards of our respective faculties for our names. This was long before smartphones and social media could deliver instant updates—back then, everything was a little slower, a little more personal, and somehow, much more real.

We boarded a taxi and made our way up to the iconic University Hill, the sun shining down on us like a silent witness to our joy. We could hardly contain our excitement.

Our first stop was the Institute of Psychology. The moment I laid eyes on the notice board, there it was—my name. Printed clearly. Bold and official. I could hardly believe it. I walked toward the office to collect my offer letter, my heart pounding with a mixture of awe, relief, and overwhelming gratitude. I had made it. I was on the list of those selected for government sponsorship.

What made it even more surreal was how few names were on the Institute of Psychology notice board. And mine was one of them.

It was a moment I will never forget.

I remember feeling incredibly special, as if I had stepped into a story much bigger than myself. It felt divine—like something had aligned beyond what I could see or orchestrate.

Irene and I then made our way to the School of Social Work and Social Administration, where she too found her name on the board. Her face lit up, and I could see the same wonder in her eyes that I felt in mine. We couldn't stop grinning as we walked away from the campus that day, our hearts full and our steps light.

Two young women, ready to take on the world, excited for the adventure unfolding before us. It felt like the beginning of everything.

CHOICES
The Hidden Cost of Freedom

When I started university, I had three years ahead of me, pursuing a degree in Community Psychology. It was a relatively new course at the time, and not many people had heard of it. It wasn't one of the typical, well-known programs like Law, Medicine, or Engineering. To be honest, it hadn't been my first choice either. I had always dreamt of studying Law. Everyone who knew me, myself included—believed I would have made an excellent lawyer.

But, as always, my father's opinion carried great weight in my decisions.

During my Senior Six second-term holiday, we had a serious conversation about my future. I shared my desire to study Law, but my father was firmly opposed to the idea. He worried about the moral dilemmas I might face as a Christian.

"How will you defend people you know are guilty of crimes like murder, robbery, or corruption?" he asked. "How will your conscience hold up if you're trained to lie so convincingly that they go unpunished? If you choose Law, you might as well forget salvation and heaven!"

It was clear that he felt strongly about it, and I didn't want to disappoint him. His suggestion instead? Theology. But I knew in my heart that wasn't the path for me. Growing up in a deeply Christian household had already felt like a theology degree in itself. I needed something different—something that resonated with me personally. I thought long and hard, because his approval meant the world to me, and Community Psychology genuinely intrigued me as a potential choice.

I told him about this new course I had discovered and explained how it could be used to make a real difference in people's lives. I painted a vision of using my training to support my sister, Sayuni, and others like her. I spoke of establishing an advocacy centre for Down syndrome, or even a home for children with disabilities, with potential support and funding from international organisations.

By the way, I still carry that passion today. The dream hasn't faded. In fact, I have land reserved specifically for this vision to be realised.

My father was moved by the idea. And to my great relief, he gave his blessing. That became my first choice.

And just like that, my journey into psychotherapy began.

Not long after the joy of the results celebration and my trip to Makerere with Irene, it was time to piece everything together—sorting accommodation, finalising my registration, and stepping into university life. As life often does, everything began to move quickly. Before I knew it, I was fully settled in—navigating lectures, assignments, deadlines, part-time work, and the social web of campus life.

I rented a shared room just below Makerere College Girls Hostel, directly across from the university. Walking to class was convenient, but what made me feel particularly clever was my entrepreneurial spirit. Instead of taking my allocated spot in Africa Hall—one of the perks of my government sponsorship—I chose to rent it out. It gave me extra income while still enjoying the comfort and flexibility of my off-campus accommodation.

It was a smart, strategic move—and one of the many ways I learned to make the most of every opportunity. The sponsorship package I received covered tuition, accommodation in Africa Hall, and a monthly upkeep allowance, which was deposited into a personal account I had to open with Postbank—a bank fully owned by the Government of Uganda. I'm not sure if things still work the same way today, but that was the system back then. I had even heard it was more generous in earlier years.

Interestingly, although I had already been working at the bookshop, all my payments had been made in cash. Opening this account felt like a significant step forward—a move toward real financial independence. It was exciting. Something empowering about holding a bank slip in my name, knowing I had a reason to manage my money.

Orientation week was a frenzy of excitement. The campus buzzed with energy every evening as students from all corners of the country came together to explore, connect, and soak up the freedom of this new chapter. We found our lecture halls, figured out our timetables, and slowly learned our way around the sprawling university grounds.

Arguably, anyone who has been to university will tell you it is one of the best times of your life. Finally, there is freedom. But as the saying goes, with great power comes great responsibility. Or in my case, I might rephrase it: with great freedom comes great confusion.

And that confusion? I was right in the thick of it.

In those first two years, I made choices—some thrilling, others reckless—that would alter the course of my life forever.

As I embarked on my journey at Makerere University, Ambrose went on to pursue Human Resources at Makerere University Business School, an extension campus located in a different area of town. At this stage, we were on very different paths—not just geographically, but emotionally too.

I was eager to experience all the excitement that university life had to offer. Nights out dancing with friends, exploring new places, and even trying things like alcohol for the first time. These were the adventures I craved. I wanted to feel alive, uninhibited, and free. Ambrose, on the other hand, was more grounded, mature, and focused. He had a way of looking at life that felt, at the time, too serious for me.

In truth, it sometimes felt like he was trying to guide me, maybe even mould me as though he were my father. I didn't want that. I wanted freedom. I wanted space to figure things out on my own terms. And while he may have meant well, the gap between us kept widening.

Eventually, we broke up.

It wasn't easy. It was the only relationship I had ever known. Letting go felt like stepping into a void I wasn't prepared for. But somewhere deep inside, I knew it was time. What I didn't know then was that walking away would throw me straight into a maelstrom of confusion.

Not long after, I found myself drawn to Alan, one of my classmates. I first noticed him in our Human Sexuality class, where he was always cracking jokes and making everyone laugh. There was something magnetic about him—charming, funny, and incredibly easy to talk to. He carried a carefree warmth, as though the world's troubles couldn't touch him. He lived fully in the moment, enjoying the here and now.

And I was hooked.

We started dating, and for a while, I truly thought I had found a healthy relationship.

But life wasn't done complicating things.

Enter Moses, another classmate. He was light-hearted, kind, and carried a unique blend of introverted depth and extroverted charm. Something was calming about his presence—gentle, yet quietly confident. He asked me out not long after Alan and I had started dating. Like me, Moses was also on a government sponsorship, something I respected and admired. It reflected discipline, ambition, and intelligence—qualities I held in high regard. But my heart was already with Alan. I told Moses this, gently but clearly, expecting that to be the end of the conversation.

Instead, he smiled—undeterred—and said, "I'll keep trying. Who knows? Maybe one day you'll change your mind."

Despite that unexpected response, things didn't become awkward. We all became good friends, and Moses quickly distinguished himself for another reason: his incredible musical talent.

He began performing at popular venues like Chez Johnson (later renamed Europe Learns About Africa) and Blue Africa at Crested Towers. Our group—Alan, Moses, and several others—often attended his shows to cheer him on.

Watching him perform was captivating. Seeing one of our own chase his dreams with such passion, boldness, and authenticity was nothing short of inspiring. Moses wasn't just a classmate or a friend anymore. He was becoming an artist in his own right—a symbol of creativity and courage at a time when many of us were still trying to find our place in the world.

Not long after that, Moses began to gain recognition. His talent caught the attention of none other than Chameleone, one of Africa's biggest stars.

I remember one evening after class, Moses was practically glowing as he shared the news. Just the day before, he had met with Chagga, who had introduced him to Chameleone and the Leone

Island crew. He was still in awe of the experience, speaking as if everything he had ever dreamed of was suddenly within reach.

At that time, Chameleone wasn't just a star. He was a phenomenon, right at the peak of his career. For Moses, meeting him was nothing short of life-changing.

It was the era of the Pearl of Africa Music Awards (PAM Awards), and I vividly remember one of those years Chameleone won but was out of the country. To everyone's surprise, he nominated Moses—now known by his stage name, Radio to accept the award on his behalf.

It was a significant moment, not only for Moses but for all of us who had witnessed his journey. We had been there in the early stages: the campus gigs, the tentative confidence, and now this achievement. After the ceremony, he joined us at TLC, which was a popular hangout back then—where friends gathered to unwind and share stories, dreams, and plans. His exhilaration was palpable, and it radiated throughout the place, igniting a shared sense of joy and inspiration among us all.

"This is just the beginning," he said.

And we all believed him.

He was right, of course.

Radio went on to become one of Uganda's greatest musical minds—a true pioneer of many changes in the industry. His music transcended boundaries, blending genres with ease and inspiring countless people with his raw talent, emotional honesty, and lyrical brilliance. Whether it was a love song, a call for unity, or a celebration of life, his voice carried a rare authenticity that connected deeply with listeners.

His demise in February 2018 was a deep and personal wound to all who knew him—and to the music world. It was like losing a rising star in mid-ascent, a brilliant force with so much more potential still to be realised. His passing left a painful void, a haunting sense of what could have been. It felt like a symphony had been cut short just before its most beautiful crescendo.

We were all grief-struck by his death. Uganda had lost a once-in-a-generation talent. We had lost a friend.

Radio wasn't just a performer. He was an exceptional songwriter, a poetic genius who could turn the most mundane words into lyrics that moved the soul. His gift was profound. He could take the everyday conversation and weave it into something musical, meaningful, and unforgettable.

And though he left us far too soon, his legacy lives on—in his music, in the memories we carry, and in the countless lives he touched along the way.

May he continue to rest in peace, forever remembered for the brilliance he shared with the world.

Now, where was I again, in my haze of reflection?

Ah yes—amidst all this, I was still working at the bookshop.

My shifts were thoughtfully arranged around my class schedule, fitting into weekends and holidays. The work kept me busy—and, in some unspoken way, grounded. While the world around me swirled with dreams, friendships, change, and even heartbreak, the bookshop remained steady. It was my quiet centre.

THE FUTURE BEGAN
Quietly, and in Disguise

It was a sunny afternoon, and I was covering Esther's lunch break at the bookshop counter when Raymond walked in. He moved with easy confidence, scanning the shelves before settling on the book he was looking for and bringing it to the counter. As we began chatting, his eyes caught on a stack of flyers advertising "Gospel Night at TLC every Thursday." His face instantly lit up.

"You're kidding," he said, holding up one of the flyers, his voice tinged with surprise and delight. "Who's behind this?"

His reaction threw me off for a moment, but I smiled and replied, "I did. My roommate and I are regulars at Gospel Night, and I'm also a member of Watoto Church."

The look on his face was priceless—equal parts admiration and disbelief. "You? This is incredible," he said, his tone warm and genuine.

Raymond was the Public Relations Manager for Power FM, the Watoto Church radio station located in the same building as the bookshop. The KPC building—now known as the Watoto Building—was a lively hub, home to the church, the radio station, and a variety of small businesses that kept the space buzzing with life.

Gospel Night, as it turned out, was one of Raymond's brainchildren—a youth outreach initiative that doubled as a stage for young Christian artists. Many of them would later become celebrated names in Uganda's gospel music scene. Seeing the flyers seemed to strike a chord in him, and as we talked about the event, I could sense how much it meant to him. What struck me more, though, was the way he spoke—his words laced with sincerity, his tone calm and steady. And then there was his smile. It wasn't just a smile; it was the smile—radiant, warm, and disarmingly genuine. It wasn't just the perfectly aligned white teeth or the way his lips curved; it was the kind of smile that seemed to come from deep within, lighting up his whole face and, somehow, the entire room.

I caught myself smiling shyly back, unable to help it. The more he spoke, the more captivated I became, my cheeks flushing in a way I couldn't quite control. Was it hormones? Was it lust? Was it just the rush of butterflies in my stomach? Perhaps. After all, I was only 21. But I didn't understand it—it was something unexpected, something I couldn't quite put into words. When he eventually left, I found myself lingering at the counter, unable to focus on much else. I dashed to the bathroom, looked at myself in the mirror, and whispered a prayer:

"God, please give me this man. I won't ask for anyone else. He's perfect in every way. He loves You, he comes from a good family, and I know my father will approve without so many questions."

Where I come from, a person's background and lineage are deeply significant. My father, a man of strong principles, valued these things immensely. At the time, he was about 80 years old, his health growing more fragile by the day. There was a constant weight in my heart—a sense of urgency to make him proud, to give him the joy of seeing me settled with a family before it was too late.

Alan, on the other hand, was everything a girl could possibly hope for. He was kind, respectful, creative, and attentive—so much so that I sometimes found myself searching for flaws just to reassure myself that no one could be that perfect. But there were none. Alan loved me sincerely, and I loved him back. We shared a warm, genuine affection, a sweetness that made our time together feel easy, even dreamlike.

And yet, for all the goodness between us, I couldn't silence a quiet voice inside that reminded me of one undeniable truth—Alan was as young as I was. He was navigating life's questions at the same pace I was, figuring out who he was and where he was going. As much as I cared for him, I knew it wasn't fair to expect from him a depth of certainty or direction that neither of us had yet fully grasped. It wasn't about a lack in him; it was about the stage we were both in—youthful, wide-eyed, and still unfolding.

With Raymond, things took on a different hue altogether. Beyond the undeniable spark of attraction—the kind that made the air feel charged every time he walked into a room—there was a weight to my feelings. A sense of grounding. He struck me as older, not just in age but in presence. He was composed, thoughtful, and mature. A Christian. A young man who seemed to know exactly where his feet stood and where he was heading.

Our worlds were not strangers to each other either. There was a network of family ties, shared histories, and long-standing respect that knit our backgrounds together like overlapping threads in a tapestry. My father knew his paternal grandfather, Canon Katugugu, and his maternal grand-uncle, Bishop Festo—two stalwart Christian leaders revered across Rujumbura. Some of Raymond's aunties had once been classmates of my older siblings. His Auntie, Joy had even stood beside my sister Damalie as a maid of honour at her wedding.

There were more profound connections too. My brother David had known Raymond's father, Reverend John, and had walked through fire—sometimes literally—with his uncle, General Jim. The two of them had forged a brotherhood during the guerilla war, surviving near-death encounters and swearing a blood pact that bound them for life. In my family, such bonds were not spoken of lightly. They ran deep, rooted in shared sacrifice and loyalty.

I didn't need to rehearse how I'd explain him to my parents or carefully defend his background. There was nothing to defend. His family already carried a quiet kind of respect—the kind you don't have to speak of because everyone recognises it. That mattered—more than I could admit at the time. Because in my world, love wasn't just about two hearts beating wildly. It was about the soil those hearts had grown from. It was about where you came from, who raised you, how you carried your name, and whether or not your futures could respectfully intertwine.

It felt like something divine was being stitched quietly into my story. Like destiny had moved a thread. And at that moment, with Raymond's smile etched into my mind like soft ink on a fresh page, I couldn't help but wonder—was this the answer to the prayer I hadn't dared speak out loud?

WHEN WANT SPEAKS LOUDER THAN WILL

There are moments in life when the heart leads, even when it knows better. Not because it doesn't hear the voice of reason or the whisper of God's will, but because desire can be blinding. Sometimes, we convince ourselves that wanting something deeply enough makes it right. That our sincerity will sanctify it. But God, in His mercy and sovereignty, does not always interrupt our choices—especially when we've made it clear that His will isn't what we're asking for.

Perhaps God heard my prayer and thought, You haven't asked for My will—only for what you want. But since you're so persistent, go on then with your want.

From that initial chat with Raymond, things unfolded naturally—or so I told myself. We began talking more and more, meeting whenever I was at work, and with each conversation, my thoughts about him deepened. He talked about the future in a way that captivated me, painting vivid pictures of what it could look like. His words carried such hope and conviction that I found myself wanting to be part of it.

He spoke so earnestly about his relationship with God, and that drew me in even more. It wasn't just his charm or the ease with which he carried himself; it was the depth in his words, the sense of purpose in his vision. Every conversation felt like a brick in a castle I was building in my mind—a castle so magnificent I never stopped to question if it was real or just infatuation. I didn't pause to think. I didn't want to think.

But what was I to tell Alan? Why would I even break up with him? How could I justify it to him—or to myself? The confusion was overwhelming. Somehow, I managed to juggle school, work, and this emotional chaos, though I often wonder now how I held it together. Being young has its way of pulling you into storms you don't even recognise until you're already drenched.

Then came 31 December 2005—a day that marked an ending I hadn't fully prepared for. Alan was out with his friends that night, and Raymond asked if I'd like to go out. I said yes. We walked into Mateos, a lively hangout in Kampala, and there he was—Alan—with his friends. Our eyes met across the room, and I froze. The air felt heavy, like the moment before a storm. I turned to Raymond and whispered, "We need to leave."

We left and headed to Steak Out, hoping to salvage the evening, but no sooner had we settled than Alan appeared. He didn't waste any time. Standing before Raymond, he demanded, "What are you doing with my girlfriend?"

Raymond, calm as ever, glanced at me and asked, "Is this your boyfriend?"

I don't know what came over me, but I looked Alan straight in the eye and said, "No."

Alan's face fell, his voice trembling as he asked, "What did you say?"

I repeated it, cold and detached: "You're not my boyfriend."

The words felt foreign even as I said them, like they belonged to someone else. Alan stood there, shattered. I could see the hurt in his eyes, the disbelief. And in that moment, I became someone

I didn't recognise—cold, heartless, and indifferent. What kind of person does this? What kind of Christian was I? What kind of love was this?

The weight of it hit me immediately. I excused myself, left, and cried all the way back to my hostel. I felt like Judas and Simon Peter rolled into one—betraying and denying someone I truly cared about. That night, I called Alan, apologised profusely, and begged him to come by just to see that I was back in my hostel. He came. He hugged me, tears streaming down his face, and told me how much I had hurt him.

For a few weeks after that, I cut ties with Raymond and focused on pleading with Alan to forgive me. And he did—at least, he tried. We saw each other on and off, but the damage was done. The trust, the connection, the easy way we used to be together—it was all gone. We never talked about what happened in detail because, really, what was there to say? Judas had done the deed, and Peter had denied knowing the one he loved. I had done them both—betrayal and denial, all wrapped into one confusing mess.

Eventually, our relationship faded away, dying quietly under the weight of what could no longer be repaired. And slowly but surely, I started talking to Raymond again. Whatever it was we had been building before—infatuation, love, or something in between—we picked up where we left off, determined to see it through.

Looking back now, I understand that God's silence was never absence. He was present through every choice, every betrayal and at every turn. He let me walk the road I insisted on, not to punish but to let me learn. And in the learning, I found grace—not just for myself, but also for those I hurt.

Because grace, after all, is not only what catches us when we fall. Sometimes, it is what follows us even when we walk away.

RIPPLES FROM VALENTINE'S DAY

I was with Raymond, but the weight of my actions haunted me. What I had done lingered like a shadow I couldn't shake. There was no excitement in this new chapter of my life—only heaviness, a sense of quiet dread.

Perhaps sensing my unease, Raymond once shared something he thought might bring comfort. He told me he had been on the verge of an engagement before meeting me. The girl had been on tour with the Watoto Children's Choir, and things had been serious between them. But then he met me—and everything changed, he said. After spending time with me and getting to know my family, he believed I was the one he truly wanted.

His words were meant to soothe, I suppose. Instead, they only unsettled me further. I couldn't shake the feeling that all of this was moving too fast, built on foundations too shaky. And beneath it all, I was still wrestling with guilt.

Valentine's Day 2006 arrived like any other day. I finished work early and attended a church event, where a Christian movie was being shown. I returned to the hostel afterwards and settled into bed.

At around 1 a.m., there was a knock at my door. It was Raymond. I let him in.

What followed that night would change my life forever.

It was the night I conceived.

A few weeks later, I missed my period. At first, I didn't think much of it. For a year or two, I had been battling hormonal issues and receiving treatment for irregular periods—thanks to Liz, whose sister had kindly added me to their medical insurance at Mayo Clinic. I had been dealing with clotting and excessive bleeding, so missing a cycle or two wasn't unusual. I even welcomed the break sometimes.

But this time was different. I began to feel unwell—tired, bloated, slightly off balance. Something in me stirred uneasily.

Eventually, I went in to get tested. My fears were confirmed: I was pregnant.

The news hit me like a tidal wave. I was consumed by panic, guilt, and an overwhelming sense of shame. This wasn't supposed to happen—not like this. I had dreams of being married, of doing things in the "right" order. Now I was facing the reality of becoming a young woman with a child and no wedding.

What would my father say? The thought of his disappointment made me physically ill. I was sure he would disown me. My mother too—what an embarrassment I had become. Everything I had imagined—the proud giveaway ceremony, the joy of walking down the aisle with dignity—felt shattered beyond repair.

I walked into the clinic one day, fully resolved to terminate the pregnancy. I told no one. I was going to fix this quietly, erase the mistake, and carry on. But as I sat there in the waiting room, numb and afraid, hesitation overwhelmed me.

Why was I doing this alone?

Why couldn't I say anything to anyone?

Why did this feel so wrong?

I couldn't go through with it. I left the clinic and returned to my hostel, trying to move through the day as if nothing had happened.

Later that afternoon, I saw Raymond and found the courage to tell him that I was pregnant. I expected anger, disappointment, or at the very least confusion. But instead, he smiled, hugged me, and said, "That is wonderful news."

His calmness unnerved me. I couldn't tell if he was truly happy or simply trying to appear strong. "I don't think it's wonderful," I muttered under my breath.

He promised to support me, but his assurance did little to ease the turmoil inside. Given how I viewed his relationship with God, I couldn't bring myself to tell him that I had considered abortion. The shame of even thinking it felt unbearable. So I stayed silent and agreed to schedule a scan.

When we went for the scan, I braced myself for more shock. And it came.

"There are two embryos, each in its own sac," the sonographer said casually, as though he were describing something entirely ordinary.

Twins.

The word echoed in my mind. Twins? I was stunned. Terrified. Speechless.

I remember thinking how close I had come to making a decision I could never undo. If I had gone through with it, would I have ever known? Would I have been told it was twins? Probably not.

And in that moment, a strange blend of relief and reverence filled me. This wasn't what I had planned. But it was now my reality. And perhaps, even then, a sliver of grace was already forming in the shadows of my fear.

A FUTURE FORGED BY HASTE AND RESOLVE

Everything unfolded rapidly after the scan. Raymond, seemingly ready to take charge of the situation, suggested that the best course of action was to get married as soon as possible. He knew my father's stance on matters like this—I had made it clear long before we found ourselves in this predicament. From conversations within his own family, Raymond also understood that this wouldn't be a casual decision for anyone involved.

So, we moved swiftly. We began arranging visits to family members to make our intentions known.

The first visit was to David and his wife, Juliet. I introduced Raymond, and to my surprise, the meeting became unexpectedly emotional. David spoke warmly about Raymond's father and uncle, reminiscing about shared experiences and long-standing connections between our families. His words were reassuring. "You've brought someone from a respected and well-known home," he said. At that moment, it already felt like family.

While David and Raymond went off to chat, I stayed behind with Juliet and confided in her about the pregnancy. She listened with the calm, steady presence I had always admired in her. Later, she and David spoke privately. A few days afterwards, David met with me again and said we needed to arrange a formal introduction with our parents—before the pregnancy became visibly obvious. We both knew what that would mean.

From that point on, the wheels were in motion.

Somewhere in the flurry of preparations, Raymond and I got engaged. There was no fancy moment, no dramatic proposal, no sparkling lights. It simply had to be done. Truthfully, I can't remember exactly where, when, or how it happened. The frenzy of emotion and urgency blurred everything. The significance of the moment was lost in the enormity of what surrounded it.

Next, we visited Patrick. Like David, he reinforced the importance of moving swiftly, knowing our parents' principles and how quickly word could spread. But Patrick didn't just give his blessing—he rolled up his sleeves and stood right beside us. He drove me and my friends around, cracked jokes, lightened my moods, and smoothed every rough edge of those stressful days. David quietly took on the role of financier, covering the requirements for the upcoming function at home.

What touched me deeply was how seamlessly my friends blended into this chapter. They already knew Patrick from our school years, and that shared history made everything feel familiar and comforting. What could have been a time of loneliness and fear became something held up by sisterhood. They surrounded me like a fortress—offering their time, resources, energy, and presence without hesitation. They travelled with me, prepared for every occasion, and stood by my side through it all.

I often say, quoting Rudyard Kipling, "I keep my friends the way misers keep their money." That rings true for me because of how deeply my friends are woven into my life.

In the midst of all the chaos, one thing stood out with clarity:

I was not alone.

Their unwavering love became the ground beneath my trembling steps. The path I had chosen wasn't easy. But it was mine.

And I had to walk it.

I must say, having my friends there with me helped shield me from the kinds of eyes that might have pried—wondering if I was pregnant, or trying to read between lines that weren't theirs to interpret. Everyone was caught up in the moment, and thankfully, no one paid too much attention to the bride. My friends knew the assignment: keep me busy, always doing something, always somewhere.

All the formalities went smoothly. My parents had invited family elders, my older siblings, and a few of their close friends. Raymond came with his close family, just as expected. It was an important cultural tradition—one that called for presence, respect, and precision. Every step, every voice, every gesture held weight. They had come to ask for my hand in marriage.

After the function, I returned to Kampala. I didn't stay at home for the usual bride pampering that often happens in the lead-up to marriage.

In Ankole culture, this is a significant and cherished rite. Brides-to-be are kept indoors, carefully nurtured by the women of the family. It is not just a time of rest, but a sacred period of preparation—of the body, spirit, and mind. A bride is fed well, nourished with milk and hearty foods meant to strengthen and soften her. Butter or ghee is applied to the skin to give it a glow. These acts, though outwardly about appearance, carry inward significance. They are rituals of readiness—of grace, dignity, and honour—as the young woman is prepared for the new life she is about to embrace.

But I chose not to take part.

The reason was painfully simple: I was afraid. I knew that if my parents discovered I was pregnant before the wedding, everything could fall apart. My father's principles were clear. His reaction would not be favourable—not in the slightest. So, I stayed away. I feared that the wedding preparations could be sabotaged, undone before they even began, if my secret came out too soon. I found myself caught between preserving a rich tradition and protecting the fragile situation I had created.

Ah, the joys and sorrows of hasty decisions.

By the end of my second year at university, I was married and pregnant—with twins. Looking back, the wedding day was far from the best day of my life. But it was a day of commitment, and I was determined to honour that commitment. More than anything, I longed for my father's approval. But that approval hung by a delicate thread—he could not find out about the pregnancy until after the wedding. If he did, he would not attend. He would not bless the union. He would never forgive what I had done.

I trusted David and Patrick to keep the truth under wraps until the ceremony was over. They understood what was at stake.

But of course, Mary—couldn't hold back. As soon as the wind blew the secret her way, she was quick to whisper it to him. She told my father I was pregnant.

And it happened as I stood at the altar.

My father, though visibly shaken, remained composed. He was caught between a rock and a hard place—too late to disown me, but unwilling to celebrate what had already happened. In the end, he made his choice: he stayed for the function, but he would not give a speech.

It was hard to swallow. But I accepted it. I couldn't have it all, could I?

Still, somewhere in the ache, I felt I had earned a part of his approval. I was now a grown woman. I had done what he asked—or at least tried. I had respected his wishes as best I could and walked a path that, in his eyes, was the "right" one.

You see, when I left for university, my parents were clear:

"You are responsible for the choices you make. If you find a man who loves you, get married. But don't fall pregnant."

And there I was—married, but pregnant.

Married to a man I believed would be accepted by my family. A man from a family my father knew and respected. But deep down, I couldn't help wondering about the man I had left behind—the one with whom marriage had never been in our immediate plans. We had been young and in love, but life had taken a different turn. And I knew my father didn't have much time left. It felt urgent, almost necessary, to give him someone he could approve of while I continued my studies.

The first phone call after the wedding came from my parents. Now that the dust had settled, they demanded answers.

"Why did you put us through this? Why did you lead us down a path of unrighteousness?"

My father's anger was unmistakable. His disappointment weighed heavily on every word.

And I had nothing to offer in return—only endless apologies, delivered with an aching heart.

This wedding was also political in every sense. And yet, against all odds, we managed to bring two families together. For a brief moment, we achieved a rare alignment, if only for a season.

PART III:

LOVE, LOSS, AND BECOMING MORE

MARRIAGE, MOTHERHOOD, AND THE BONDS THAT SUSTAINED ME

Soon after our wedding on August 5th, 2006, we settled into married life. I was just 22 years old, stepping into a new chapter with all the optimism of a young bride. Raymond, at 26, embraced the responsibilities of being a husband with quiet resolve and care.

Thanks to the *okuhingira*—a traditional Ankole giveaway ceremony where the bride's family blesses the couple with essentials to start their home—we began our life together with everything we needed. My family had gifted us an array of items: household furniture, kitchen necessities, bedding, and more. The practice of *okuhingira* symbolises the bride's family's support and well-wishes, providing a strong foundation upon which the couple can build their life together.

It was a meaningful tradition—one I appreciated deeply.

As I entered my final trimester, I took time off from my job at the bookshop. My body was heavy, my energy low, and I was preparing for the arrival of two little lives. The transition into adulthood had been swift—but motherhood came crashing in faster and harder than I ever imagined.

Despite the generous gifts and the support we received, life was anything but easy. I was in my third year of university, heavily pregnant, and carrying twins for the first time. It was an overwhelming season—a convergence of academic pressure, physical exhaustion, and emotional vulnerability.

But I was not alone.

I was blessed with the unwavering support of my dear friends, Alice and Phiona T. They stood by me in ways that still move me to this day. They ensured I stayed on track with coursework, helped secure my exam timetables, and supported me through preparations for tests and assignments. Their kindness extended well beyond academics. They visited me often, bringing snacks to satisfy my pregnancy cravings and groceries to help ease the burden at home. Their presence was deeply reassuring.

My friendship with Alice began at Mpoma School, though interestingly, I first became close with her sister, Milly. Milly and I were in the same sub-class and slept in the same dormitory. We quickly bonded over the little things that mean so much in school life. At one point, we even kept our snacks in the same suitcase—a common boarding school tradition we fondly called "sharing grab," where close friends pooled all their treats into one case, while the other suitcase was reserved strictly for clothes. With Alice, the bond formed differently. We were drawn together by our shared love for literature—reading novels, discussing characters, and writing creative pieces. That mutual passion became the foundation of a lasting connection. If I recall correctly, we even represented the school at a creative writing competition and won an award. Though we went to different A' level schools—Alice to Iganga Girls and I to Namirembe Hillside—life brought us back together at university. Remarkably, we ended up on the same course, both on government sponsorship, and what began in the dormitories of Mpoma rekindled into something even deeper.

Alice and I shared countless small yet meaningful moments that stitched our lives more tightly together. I vividly recall how, during our O'level vacation, she took me to get my ears pierced. It may seem like a simple thing, but for me, it was a lasting symbol of our sisterhood—bold, memorable, and shared. Even when she didn't agree with some of my choices, Alice never judged me. She offered support, choosing empathy over criticism, and love over opinion. Her friendship was—and still is—one of the purest gifts I received during those years.

And then there was Phiona T—not to be confused with the earlier Phiona I mentioned, but another invaluable friend. We met at university, and to this day, I can't quite recall when or how it began. It's one of those rare friendships that forms organically, without effort or explanation. Somewhere along the way, we grew so close that she would later stand beside me as one of my bridesmaids.

Phiona offered her friendship without conditions and her support without needing to be asked. Through all the challenges I faced, she remained a steady, gentle source of strength. Her loyalty, calmness, and quiet encouragement reminded me that sometimes the most powerful love is the one that simply stays.

BORN OF TWO, HELD BY ONE

When I delivered my firstborns—a pair of twins—on 7 November 2006, joy and sorrow arrived hand in hand. It had been a challenging pregnancy in more ways than I can count: physically, emotionally, financially, and spiritually. I was stretched in every direction. Carrying twins was no small feat, especially as I balanced the demands of university, a young marriage, and the looming uncertainties of motherhood. I was exhausted; my body ached constantly. Yet I held on with hope and fervent prayers, believing that somehow it would all be worth it in the end.

Labour was no less difficult. I endured an entire night and morning of intense, unrelenting pain. There were moments when I felt as though my body was being torn apart, but I kept waiting, believing that the finish line was near. By early afternoon, though, it was clear something was terribly wrong. An emergency caesarean section was ordered around 3 p.m., but it came too late.

My daughter was born a macerated stillbirth.

I hadn't even held her alive. I never heard her cry. Never felt her breath on my skin. She slipped into this world quietly—and quietly she was taken. Yet her absence thundered through me like a storm, piercing me in a place I didn't know existed. The grief was immediate—swift, sharp, consuming.

There is no language for the sorrow of losing a child you carried—a child you dreamed about, talked to, and loved long before you met her. I had imagined their first smiles, matching outfits, and the beauty of raising twins. Suddenly, half of that dream lay shattered.

And still, there was no time to truly grieve. My son was alive—fragile, precious, utterly dependent on me. He needed me. So, with a body still healing and a heart still bleeding, I moved forward on autopilot: one part of me mourning the daughter I had lost, the other determined to be present for the son I still had.

I will never forget the silence in that hospital room when I woke up. It was the kind of silence that screams. Nurses came and went, hushed voices passing between them, but I felt underwater—floating between joy and despair. I had given birth to two...and would only be taking one home.

To this day, I don't know how I survived that moment, except by God's grace. A God who sees, who stays, who carries us when we can no longer carry ourselves—a God who, even in death, was near.

But gratitude doesn't erase the grief. The loss of my daughter remains a silent ache, tucked beneath my everyday strength. I never got to watch her grow. Never got to know the sound of her laughter or the shape of her dreams. She is the silence in a conversation, the empty space beside her brother. I carried her in my womb, and now I carry her in my heart—a wound invisible to most, but never far from the surface.

With the demands of school, marriage, and motherhood, I had no choice but to move forward. My days were consumed with trying to be a good wife, a capable student, and a nurturing mother. There was no time to dwell on the future; I could only focus on the immediate tasks in front of me. I hoped that somehow, everything else would fall into place.

And so, the days blurred into one another—holding a baby in one arm, clutching hope in the other, while trying to hold together a home that was already quietly fraying at the seams.

As I navigated these challenges, cracks began to appear in our marriage.

Raymond, beneath the surface of his charming words and lofty promises, struggled with the realities of life. By the time we married, he had already lost his job at the radio station—long before the wedding—and had remained unemployed since. While his intentions may have been good, his actions, or more accurately his inaction, told a different story.

He wasn't actively looking for work. He dismissed most opportunities that came his way and increasingly withdrew from the responsibilities piling up around us. To make matters worse, he belittled my efforts. He mocked my job at the bookshop, brushing it off as insignificant. But to me, that job—however small—was a huge blessing to have.

The castles he had built in my mind with his words began to crumble.

The weight of new motherhood, financial strain, and the daily work of managing a household were slowly breaking me. I was exhausted—physically, emotionally, and spiritually. But life doesn't pause, and neither could I. I spoke to Auntie Charity, explaining that I needed to resume work earlier than planned. She understood.

My early return took some of my colleagues by surprise. They thought it was too soon, especially after the complications with the birth. But Freshvine had been there for me in different seasons of my life, and this time was no different. Work gave me something to focus on—a small escape from what was unfolding at home.

The bookshop brought some structure back to my days. But the truth was, the income was so modest that it was nearly all swallowed up by transport costs. Living in Kisaasi, far from the city centre, meant I was often working just to afford the commute.

Amidst the struggles, a few rays of hope continued to shine through.

One of them was Raymond's friend, David—affectionately known as Dodi by his family and close friends. He became a pillar of support during one of the most difficult seasons of our lives.

David didn't just celebrate with us—he made the celebration possible. He had offered us the wedding venue at Calendar Hotel completely free of charge, a gesture that had lifted a huge weight from our shoulders. His kindness didn't stop there. After the wedding, he continued to support us in thoughtful ways. David often visited us at our home in Kisaasi, bringing gifts for the baby—most notably, tins of SMA formula. At a time when this particular baby milk formula was prohibitively expensive, his generosity was nothing short of a lifeline. Knowing I wouldn't have to worry about milk for a week or two brought immense relief. It was a kindness I never took for granted.

But even these moments of help, gracious and heartfelt as they were, couldn't mask the growing weight of our reality.

That first year of marriage was an unrelenting storm of challenges: the round-the-clock demands of new parenthood, the strain of financial instability, and the emotional toll of unfulfilled promises and unspoken disappointments.

It became clear that we couldn't continue like this. Raymond needed to find work—urgently. He had to step up and take responsibility for his family. I could no longer bear the weight of everything on my own.

The pressure was mounting, and so were the questions.

We began to wonder: Where were all the people who had celebrated with us on our wedding day? The ones who had made promises, offered blessings, and praised us for doing things "the right way"? Where were the politicians, the well-known relatives, and their influential friends who had assured us of their support?

Their words, once warm and full of hope, now felt like hollow reverberations.

In those early days, we had clung to those assurances, believing that this network of encouragement would help us find our footing. But as reality set in, we discovered that good intentions rarely paid the rent. The applause had faded, and so had the support.

We were on our own.

During that time, it felt like we were on the same team—striving toward a shared goal, bound by a sense of purpose, and holding on to each other through the strain. Even amid difficulty, there were moments when unity felt possible. We weren't perfect, but we were trying. Yet, as the days turned into months, and the months stretched into more silence, more stress, and more distance, doubts began to grow louder. I found myself questioning the very foundation of my marriage. Was it truly built on love, or had it been held together by external forces? Expectations. Appearances. The pressure to conform to societal standards. Had we chosen each other freely, or had we been swept along by a script we never paused to rewrite?

From the very beginning, our journey had been marked by hardship. It felt as though we had entered marriage already carrying more than we could bear. And now, I began to wonder: can this marriage truly thrive in the shadow of constant strain?

Had it all been infatuation? A fleeting emotion I had mistaken for something deeper?

These questions lingered in my mind, surfacing in the quiet hours when everything else was still. I began to notice how differently we viewed partnership. I longed for shared responsibility, emotional presence, and mutual effort. But what I was met with felt more like withdrawal than companionship.

There was never really a moment to stop and consider what we truly felt for each other. Things had happened so fast—I'm certain I never gave myself the chance to ask if I loved him, or if he loved me. If love was there at all, I told myself it would grow over time. But really, what was love if not also the hope of pleasing my father?

Was I chasing an illusion rather than facing reality? The answers came—answers I didn't like but had to accept. I remembered how it had all started and how we'd arrived here: my prayers for this man rather than God's will, how I had left Alan the way I did, and my hope for my father's approval by bringing someone familiar into our lives.

I had the answers—many of them—but they brought little comfort.

But there was no time to dwell on these thoughts. As heavy as they were, they felt almost trivial compared to the daily challenges before me. I didn't have the luxury to reflect. There was a baby who needed care, bills that wouldn't wait, and the constant pressure to keep our fragile life afloat.

Whatever the reason for our marriage—love, duty, or a desire to honour my father's dreams—it no longer mattered. We were here. I was a wife and a mother, bound by the life we had built, however uncertain or strained it felt. In that moment, survival took precedence over sentiment.

As our marriage began to fray under the relentless pressure of unmet expectations and growing responsibilities, our son, Joshua, continued to grow. He was the thread holding me together—the living reminder that even in loss, something had been preserved.

Then came a moment of light amidst the shadows: his baptism.

It felt like a sacred interruption in the chaos. A milestone that held weight beyond tradition—a moment of dedication, hope, and anchoring grace. In a season where so much felt uncertain, this simple ceremony offered something pure, something deeply meaningful. It reminded me that while much was unravelling, not all was lost.

We named him Joshua, a name chosen by Raymond, and Andwanaho, a name given by my mother. In Runyankore, Andwanaho means 'He fights for me'—a powerful declaration of divine grace and protection. It was more than just a name; it was a prayer and a prophecy.

Joshua had survived what no child should ever have to endure. He had spent an estimated week in my womb alongside his twin sister, Leah, who had passed before birth. Dr Batwaala, after examining her macerated body, estimated that Leah had died approximately seven days before delivery. The weight of that reality never left me—one child went in silence, the other born into a world already carrying the memory of loss.

To honour his heritage, Joshua's paternal great-grandmother, Eva Katugugu, added the name Kabanza, meaning "the first twin." Raymond paid tribute to his late great-grandfather by giving him the name Samuel, after Canon Samuel Katugugu.

Joshua Andwanaho Kabanza Samuel—each name a layer of legacy, each one telling part of his story before he could speak it for himself.

We celebrated the baptism at our home, gathering friends and family who had walked alongside us on our journey. It was a day of joy, filled with laughter, delicious food, and heartfelt conversations. Yet, beneath the celebration, the weight of our struggles was palpable. Life felt heavier with each passing day, and we found ourselves running out of options.

SWALLOWING PRIDE, FINDING A WAY

Desperate for stability, we turned to some of Raymond's well-connected relatives, hoping their influence could open doors for us. But the results were discouraging.

Before Joshua was born, I vividly remember one incident in my last trimester. Juggling work and school while relying on public transport had become increasingly risky. Raymond approached a general—a well-connected relative—to request a car to ease my daily commute.

The general laughed off the request, saying, "How can I give you a car when you can't afford fuel? And if I give you the car, will you be asking for fuel as well?" His words stung—a blunt reminder of our struggles.

On another occasion, Raymond asked his paternal aunt—whose husband held a diplomatic post abroad—if we could stay in their guest quarters while we sorted out our housing, as we were struggling to pay rent. She declined, explaining it wasn't possible and that she didn't want to complicate family relationships.

Each rejection chipped away at our hope.

After exhausting every possible option on Raymond's side, I knew what had to be done—even though it was one of the hardest steps I would ever have to take.

Asking for help from my family felt like confirming their worst fears: that I had rushed into marriage without fully considering the practical realities of life. That I had leapt with hope, not wisdom. Raymond was still unemployed, and our situation had grown dire. But pride couldn't pay bills, and disappointment couldn't feed a child.

My brother David had already stepped in once before. He had generously paid the hospital bill for Joshua and Leah's delivery, carrying us through a moment too heavy for words. And now, in desperation, I returned to him, laying out the truth plainly—the weight of our struggles, the silence from the promises made to us, and the urgency of our need.

David didn't flinch.

He immediately reached out to a friend named Kellen, whose company, ASKAR, had secured a subcontract with EODT, a U.S.-based firm providing personnel for projects in Iraq. The opportunity came suddenly, unexpectedly—like an open door in a long hallway of closed ones.

A SWIFT UNFOLDING AND DIVINE AIRWAVES

I had always believed that God makes a way where there seems to be none, but I didn't expect the way to come wrapped in desert winds and distant borders. The job was far from ordinary—contract work in Iraq. Dangerous. Demanding. But it was an answer, and we were desperate for one.

That same week, Raymond received a call from David with what would become life-changing news: he had been accepted into the program. There would be a mandatory two-week intensive training, followed by immediate deployment with the next group of recruits.

In a matter of weeks, we shifted from scraping for rent to preparing for an international deployment.

Everything moved fast—almost too fast to process.

And just like that, Raymond was gone—stepping into a new chapter none of us had fully prepared for.

The house felt different in his absence. Quieter, but not in a sorrowful way. It was the silence of adjustment, of uncertainty, and of something finally beginning to move.

I remained behind to care for Joshua, still only a baby, with the daily help of our housemaid, Berna, and the loyal companionship of our German Shepherd, Sisqó. His protective presence gave me a small sense of comfort and stability.

There were still challenges, of course—many of them. But for the first time in a long while, there was a glimmer of hope.

We could finally begin to breathe again. Bills could be paid. Groceries could be bought without anxiety. We could manage the household without stretching every coin until it frayed. And for once, we could start to imagine a future that wasn't always tethered to fear and lack.

Then, just a few weeks later, while I was at work at the bookshop, something unexpected happened.

The Marketing and Sales Manager of Lighthouse Television (LTV), a man named David S., had come to meet Auntie Charity to discuss a potential partnership. He was hoping FreshVine would consider advertising on LTV. While waiting upstairs for his appointment—since Auntie Charity was out for lunch—he struck up a casual conversation with James, the accountant.

I was nearby when I overheard something that made my heart leap.

David S. mentioned that LTV was looking for a presenter for a brand-new gospel show sponsored by MTN. A spark lit inside me. I knew in my spirit—this was an opportunity I couldn't let slip by. I walked over, introduced myself, and asked about the role. He seemed intrigued by my presence and enthusiasm. Right there and then, he scheduled an interview for that Saturday at the station. He explained that I would need to audition, and if all went well, I'd record the show immediately—it was set to air Monday night at 9:30 p.m.

And just like that, everything began to shift.

I got the role.

Hosting a gospel show truly stirred my soul. I had the privilege of interviewing some of the country's most beloved gospel artists—exploring their journeys, highlighting their music, and promoting their upcoming events. It was more than just a platform; it was a ministry. I felt deeply aligned with its purpose.

I even had the honour of representing MTN, our show's primary sponsor. It was surreal to witness doors opening where there had once only been walls.

Suddenly, life felt brighter.

After so many struggles and empty wallets, we had found not just survival, but the early stirrings of something greater. We had stumbled into the beginnings of stability—maybe even purpose. And for the first time in a long while, I allowed myself to hope that perhaps we were on a path to thriving, not merely enduring.

Looking back on that season of my life, I carry with me a deep and quiet sense of gratitude. Gratitude for the breakthroughs. For the unexpected doors that opened. For the strength that carried me when I didn't know I had any left.

But I also carry the weight of regret.

There are choices I made that, if I'm honest, I would approach differently today. Moments when I wish I had slowed down, asked more questions, prayed longer, or simply waited. Decisions I should have made with more care and discernment.

Still, life doesn't come with a manual. There's no rulebook for how to love, how to survive hardship, how to hold a family together—or how to keep your soul from unravelling in the process. Every choice carries consequences. Every chapter writes itself in real-time.

Life is trial and error—a fragile unfolding of lessons, many of which come not in moments of clarity, but in the rubble left behind when things don't go as we hoped. We stumble before we find our footing. We break before we know how strong we truly are.

And sometimes, the lessons that shape us most are the ones that hurt the deepest.

Yet even in regret, there is redemption.

Even in mistakes, there is meaning.

A BRIEF VACATION

After some time, Berna bid me farewell. She was ready to move on, to carve out her path and pursue her dream of starting a small business. I was happy for her. She had become like family, and though I wished her well, her absence left a noticeable gap in our little household.

Not long after, I welcomed a new helper, Namitala, whose calm presence and capable hands gently restored rhythm to our days.

Time, as it always does, continued its steady march forward.

Days turned into weeks. Weeks blurred into months.

And then—finally—Raymond returned home for his first vacation since leaving for Iraq.

I still remember the emotion of that moment vividly. The embrace felt like home, the way our arms locked like puzzle pieces that had been apart for too long. There was a sense of relief in simply being in the same room again, breathing the same air, no longer separated by oceans, time zones, and the unknown.

We talked for hours about home, about Iraq, about the world that had continued spinning while we had been apart. Our conversations flowed like a stream long dammed up, released with ease and laughter. The sound of our voices, and the stories we shared, filled the house with life and light, in a way it hadn't felt for so long.

And then there was Joshua.

He had grown to know his father's voice through the phone—familiar, yes, but distant. But now, here was Dad in the flesh, reaching out, smiling, holding him close. I watched the light return to Joshua's eyes, and my heart could hardly take it. His joy was contagious, and in that moment, all the heaviness we had carried seemed to lift. It wasn't like when Raymond had left—when our home had been shadowed by lack, uncertainty, and worry.

This was different.

Our home felt lighter now. Stronger. Hopeful. Raymond's presence brought with it a sense of fullness, a reminder of what it meant to be together. And though we knew the holiday would be painfully short, we cherished every second.

It was lovely to have him back.

Even for just a little while.

Time has a way of softening edges, gently reminding us of what truly matters. Distance had, indeed, made the heart grow fonder. After so much time apart, the reunion felt like a balm. The relentless struggles that had once consumed us now seemed lighter. We savoured those precious days together as a family, aware that this moment of peace might be as fleeting as it was sweet—likely to be the best we'd have for a long time. It was a brief season of closeness, a pocket of serenity in a life otherwise marked by stretches of separation.

So much had changed since Raymond had left.

The home now ran smoothly, with bills paid on time, no longer accompanied by the panic that used to follow every utility notice. I had transitioned from working at the bookshop to staying home with Joshua while Raymond was away. And then, I embraced something new: presenting a weekly gospel television show on LTV. The pay wasn't extravagant, but the opportunity was a gift. It gave me purpose and allowed me the flexibility to raise my son. With only one day of recording required each week, I could balance work and motherhood.

But just as quickly as Raymond had returned, he had to leave again.

His vacation ended just days before my graduation—a moment I had long dreamed of, worked tirelessly for and fought to reach. It broke both of our hearts that he wouldn't be there to witness it. We had come such a long way, and it felt almost unfair that he would miss this significant milestone.

Yet, the reality of our situation was undeniable.

We needed the job. We needed the income. Sacrifices had to be made, and this was one of them. He returned to duty.

GRADUATION

Though Raymond couldn't be there, my parents were present on my graduation day. Their love filled every corner of that moment with pride, warmth, and joy.

It was an emotional milestone—a culmination of years defined by sacrifice, struggle, endurance, and unwavering determination. The path had been anything but smooth. There were seasons I didn't think I would make it. Moments when life's weight nearly buckled my knees. Sleepless nights. Juggling work, study, marriage and motherhood. The heartache of loss. The ache of distance.

And yet, by God's grace, I had made it.

I had finished what I started. I had crossed the finish line.

As I stood there in my cap and gown, the sun high and my spirit lifted even higher, I whispered a quiet thank you to God—for the strength to push through, for the silent miracles along the way, for every door He opened when I thought there were none.

What made it all even more profound was having my father there to witness it. That was the icing on the cake. He had seen me at my weakest, cheered me through my beginnings, stood by me in silence and prayer—and now he was watching me rise. I remember standing there and thinking, *If he goes now, I will be content. I've made him proud.*

And my mother—though a woman of few words and seldom one to show emotion—couldn't hide what this moment meant to her. This quiet triumph betrayed her pride. I saw it in her eyes, in the way she held her posture, in the brief, satisfied smile that flickered across her face. All the plans she had made for my education, the bold decision to send me to Kampala, the countless sacrifices to give me a fair go—all of it had led to this.

She had fought for me to have a place in the city when few believed in the dream. She endured the rejections, shouldered the anxieties, and carried the fear that maybe, just maybe, this moment might never come. But here it was. And in that instant, all of it vanished—replaced by a quiet joy, the kind that only a mother who has warred in silence for her child can understand.

My graduation was more than an academic achievement. It was a moment of triumph, gratitude, and deep reflection. A resounding reminder that, no matter how winding the road had been, perseverance and faith had brought me to this moment.

I crossed that stage with my heart full and my spirit grounded. I had finished what I started.

I was crowned in grace.

REBUILDING ON SHIFTING GROUND

As time went on, the long separation began to take its toll on Raymond. The distance once bearable because of duty and necessity, became a burden too heavy to carry. He missed home. He missed Joshua. He missed the ordinary rhythms of family life, the comfort of familiar spaces, and the sound of laughter not filtered through a phone line.

Around that time, tragedy struck his camp. One of his colleagues at Camp Shield in Iraq lost their life. I believe that moment shook him deeply. It was a stark reminder of mortality, a quiet confrontation with how fragile life is—especially when living in unfamiliar territory, under the constant shadow of danger. The combination of emotional distance, physical exhaustion, and the trauma of witnessing death up close began to unravel something inside him.

He confided in his paternal aunt, Dora, who lived in the United States at the time. In their conversation, she offered him simple but profound advice:

"Marriage is like a house; you build it best on site."

Taking her words to heart, Raymond made the life-altering decision to terminate his contract and return home for good. He arrived in August 2008, and with him came the hope of starting over—rebuilding not just our home, but perhaps also ourselves.

But that hope was soon met with reality.

Not long after his return, I began to notice that he was struggling—perhaps to adjust, or perhaps because something inside him had changed. The man who had left joyful, hopeful, outgoing, brimming with vision and faith, did not return in the same form. What came back was someone quieter, heavier, more guarded.

At first, I tried to dismiss it as the natural difficulty of readjusting to life after being away. But over time, it became clear that this was deeper. Perhaps it was the untold stories of war, the psychological toll of living in a high-risk zone, or the quiet trauma of navigating fear and isolation without the grounding of home.

Whatever the cause, the change was undeniable.

Raymond, once the man who loved jokes and light-hearted banter, began to change in ways I couldn't explain. He became easily angered, often withdrawn or anxious. His questions came suddenly and often, sometimes several times a day:

"Where were you?"

"Who did you speak to?"

"Why didn't you answer your phone?"

Our conversations, which used to be full of laughter, shared plans, and a closeness I never had to explain, started to feel like interviews. There was a sharpness in the way he spoke, as though he was trying to catch me out. It wasn't just confusing—it was painful. This wasn't the Raymond I knew.

Something had shifted, though I couldn't quite name it at the time.

Looking back now, I can see those moments for what they were: warning signs.

Subtle at first, but constant. Like the quiet hum of something not quite right.

The ground beneath me was already starting to feel unsteady, but I hadn't realised it yet. We'd faced challenges before—tight finances, distance, loss, and grief. I'd had private moments of doubt over the years, but through everything, I believed one thing without question: that Raymond was my friend. That I could talk to him about anything. That even when things were hard, I could still trust him with the truth of my heart.

But even that was beginning to slip away.

And you'd think—given my training in psychology—that I would have recognised the signs. That I'd try to get us to talk more deeply. That I'd suggest therapy. Or at least stop and take a closer look at what was going on. Maybe even do some sort of informal assessment.

You would think so.

But there's something about being personally involved—emotionally invested—that makes it hard to see clearly.

You don't respond as a professional. You respond as a person.

And when you love someone, or believe you do, you make excuses. You minimise things. You hold onto hope.

I didn't know it then, but we were slowly heading into a space we might not come back from.

Drifting from the kind of marriage we had once talked about with excitement. From the future we had imagined and prayed for.

And no training—no matter how good—can prepare you for the quiet, confusing sadness of losing something you're still holding onto.

And then, things began to spiral fast.

Raymond's comings and goings became unpredictable. He was often absent, and when he returned, he was different—distant, restless, irritable. And then came the shock: he had started drinking. Not just occasionally, but frequently and heavily.

It felt like I was watching someone unravel in front of me—someone I knew, yet now barely recognised.

With the drinking came a volatile temper. The smallest things triggered explosive reactions. He grew increasingly unpredictable. One moment calm, the next consumed by anger. And then came the threats, the accusations, and the words that cut deep.

He accused me of things I hadn't even imagined—casting doubt not just on my loyalty, but on the very fabric of our family.

Everything I had built, everything I had nurtured, was suddenly under suspicion.

It wasn't just the loss of peace; it was the loss of safety and emotional refuge. The man who had once made me feel seen and heard now made me feel like a stranger in my own home.

And though I didn't know how far things would go, I knew, deep down, that we were no longer standing on the same ground.

He questioned the paternity of our son, Joshua, and—would you believe it? —even the pregnancy I was carrying. Oh yes, I hadn't mentioned that yet, had I? Soon after his return, I conceived our second child. What should have been a joyous moment in our lives became shrouded in doubt and hostility.

When I told him the news, I expected at the very least, a flicker of joy or surprise. But instead, he looked at me, stunned, and said, "It's too soon. How could that be?"

His words cut deep.

The pregnancy felt like a crime I was being made to defend. His doubt was so deep, so entrenched, that at one of my antenatal checkups, he asked the doctor to calculate the weeks of conception to verify the timing and determine whether the child could truly be his.

I was horrified. Embarrassed. Crushed.

But it didn't stop there.

I will never forget one evening. We were on our way home when he turned to me and said something that I can still hear, word for word:

"Swear on this baby—that if you lose it, it means it was never mine."

I was speechless.

I had no words. Just silent tears and the weight of a heart breaking in slow motion.

His suspicion didn't stop with me.

He became increasingly paranoid about everyone around me, especially his friends and any male acquaintances I had known before. He questioned my friendships, my conversations, and even my expressions of kindness. He cast shadows over everything I said or did. To say his accusations were baseless would be an understatement. He conjured entire narratives in his mind and believed them as truth. Stories without logic. Accusations without evidence.

And still, I tried to reason with him. I prayed. I pleaded.

But it was like speaking to someone who had vanished. In his place stood someone I barely recognised: a man consumed by anger, suspicion, and fear.

It was devastating to watch him come undone like that—to see mistrust slowly eat away at the foundation of what I believed we had. To feel him slip further and further from the values he once upheld, the friendship we once cherished, and the faith he once professed.

Time passed in this unpredictable haze—a constant storm of tension and mistrust. I found myself slowly withdrawing, emotionally drained and spiritually exhausted. Part of me had resigned to the way he was treating me, telling myself that if I just endured it, things might return to normal.

Until one night when everything changed. That night, things fell apart.

I remember it as vividly as the break of dawn. We had spent the day at his sister Priscilla's traditional give-away ceremony, where he was officiating as the master of ceremonies. He drowned himself in the merriment, but as the festivities stretched on, it became clear that the wine had taken over. He drank far too much, and my repeated pleas to leave before he completely lost his dignity fell on deaf ears.

For hours, I found myself whispering the same exhausted phrase every time he came by where I was seated: "Please let me take you home... you're embarrassing yourself."

This upset him so much that he would just walk away.

Balancing a tired toddler on my lap and heavily pregnant, I was at my wit's end. Eventually, he agreed—but only grudgingly, insisting that once he dropped us off, he'd return to the party.

Hearing this, his brother Ronald asked him not to drive. When he wouldn't listen, Ronald chose to ride with us.

All the way home, he kept going on about how disrespectful I was.

"where did you get the authority to talk to me like that? To decide for me when enough is enough? Who do you think you are?"

I stayed quiet, knowing that saying anything in my defence would only anger him more. And really, who tries reasoning with someone in that state?

As soon as we arrived home, Raymond jumped into the driver's seat, determined to head back out. Ronald quickly intervened, pleading with him not to drive.

"You've had too much—just stay, please," he insisted, stepping in front of the car, trying to reason with him.

But something had taken hold of Raymond.

He was intoxicated—not just with alcohol, but with a rage that made him unreachable. It was as though he was driven by something darker and volatile.

Logic couldn't touch him. Words didn't land. He wasn't listening—not to Ronald, not to me, not even to his own better judgement.

The man behind the wheel that night wasn't the one we knew. He was consumed—by fury, frustration, and something far heavier than either of us could name in that moment.

Without another word, he sped off into the night, leaving me behind with our sleeping son and the growing heaviness of what I had begun to fear.

Barely ten minutes later, I heard the sound that would make my heart stop: the screech of tyres outside the gate. He was back.

But this was not a calm return.

Instead of waiting for the gate to be opened, he climbed over it, like a man unhinged, fuelled by something wild and untethered. There was no gentleness, no hesitation—just fury, boiling over.

He stormed toward the house with the ferocity of a starved lion, his rage like a fire licking at the edges of everything it touched. There was no reasoning with him now. Whatever storm had been brewing within him had broken loose.

He kicked down the door.

Before I could even process what was happening, he was on me—a storm of fists, fury, and chaos.

His blows collided with my face, my arms, and my protruding belly—each strike punctuated by words that sliced even deeper than the pain.

"Why did you lock the gate?"

"Why are you so disrespectful?"

"Why did you embarrass me at the party?"

"What's wrong with you?"

I tried to speak—to explain, to defend myself—but he couldn't hear me. In that moment, it was as if my voice didn't exist, as if he were deaf to anything but his own rage. My attempts to shield my belly only seemed to provoke and inflame him more.

"I don't care about this pregnancy!" he spat, eyes wild.

"Lose it if you want—it's not mine anyway!"

He struck my face again and again until I tasted blood, sharp and metallic on my tongue. I wasn't sure if my front teeth were still there. My body gave out—I felt a rush of warmth between my legs as blood and urine spilled together, fear forcing everything loose. But even then, there was no time to process shame.

Battered, shaking, and terrified, I clutched my belly, as though my arms could shield the life inside me from the man trying to destroy it. The same man who once made me swear that a miscarriage would prove the child wasn't his—now seemed determined to make that prophecy come true.

Joshua lay asleep in the next room, untouched by the storm exploding beyond his dreams. I stared at the door. I couldn't stay.

Something fierce and primal rose within me— an instinct beyond fear. I had to run.

Then came a moment—a gap in his fury, a stumble in his drunken pace. As he turned to grab something, I slipped beneath his arm, ducking low and moving fast, before he could register what had happened. I was gone.

In a thin nightdress, barefoot and trembling, I burst into the night. Cold air slapped my skin. My heart hammered in my chest, every beat filled with panic. I didn't know where I was going or how far I could make it. I only knew I had to get away—away from him, the violence, the house that had turned into a war zone.

All I could do was run—and pray I'd survive.

I ended up at the local trading centre, hiding in the shadows between closed shops and trees, barefoot and shaking. The night was cold and lonely, the kind that creeps into your bones. Everything felt frozen. Empty. Not a soul in sight.

I clutched my belly, praying under my breath—desperate for safety, for something to hold me together. I could barely feel my legs. My mouth tasted of metal, and my jaw ached with every breath. But what scared me more was what I couldn't see—what I couldn't protect.

"Please, God," I whispered. "Don't let me lose this baby. Not like this."

I didn't know what to do. I stood there, lost, trying to steady my breath, until I found the nerve to knock on one of the shopkeeper's doors. I knew her just a little. She opened slowly, eyes wide, and began to ask what had happened. I begged her—"Please, just let me make a call. I'll explain after."

I tried Patrick first. No answer. His phone was off. Typical—when you need someone the most.

Then I tried Beth—his sister. Hers was one of the few numbers I knew by heart. My voice was cracked and shaky, but she understood. Within minutes, Beth and Priscilla, the bride-to-be, came rushing to meet me.

Priscilla took me home with her. I spent the night there—numb, shaken, and barely holding it together. Every part of me ached, but what consumed my heart more than the pain was the silent fear for the baby. I didn't tell her what I was most worried about. I couldn't. Instead, I quietly placed my trust in God, clinging to the only hope I had left. I remember sitting still, tears welling up, whispering under my breath, *"You can't let Yourself down. You know what's on the line here. Show Yourself. Please, Lord—let this be a full-term pregnancy. Let this child be safe and whole."*

I must've said it a hundred times—over and over in my head, in my heart, in half-formed mumbles through trembling lips. The bleeding had stopped, which gave me a sliver of hope, but the fear still hovered.

Priscilla, to her credit, did what she could. She ran me a warm shower, made me a hot cup of tea, and sat with me. Her voice was soft as she tried to comfort me, her eyes filled with stunned disbelief. "I'm so sorry," she said more than once. "I don't know what's going on with him... I'm so sorry." There was something sincere in the way she said it, and I was grateful—not just for her words but for the safety of her home at such a time and on such a night.

I wrapped myself in that warmth as best I could, even if my body and soul felt bruised. I thought about what could have happened—how close it had all come. If I hadn't run... if he hadn't stumbled... if he had caught me before I got out. It chilled me to think of it. And yet, I was alive. The baby was still with me, at least for now. And in that fragile, uncertain space, I held on to hope like it was all I had left.

That night marked the end of whatever I thought I understood.

What I witnessed wasn't just a man drunk. It was something else. Wild. Animal. Something I'll never forget.

Early the next morning, I used Priscilla's phone to try Patrick again. His number had been unreachable the night before—one more weight added to an already crushing night. This time, he answered. I didn't have the strength to say much. I gave him the address and simply asked if he could come. "I'll explain when you get here," I said, my voice barely steady. He didn't hesitate.

When he arrived at Priscilla's, I was relieved to see a familiar face—but I couldn't bring myself to speak freely in front of her. She had shown me kindness, yes, but her bloodline tethered her to the man who had done this to me, and my guard couldn't drop in her presence. Patrick must have noticed the unease in my eyes. Quietly, gently, he suggested we go to his place. I nodded.

At his home, for the first time in hours, I let my body exhale. I stayed there for a while—safe, but far from okay. My face was sore, my ribs ached, and my thoughts were a tangled mess. I sat still, hands curled protectively around my belly, every now and then glancing at the clock, thinking of Joshua.

My son. My baby boy. Still in that house—with a man I no longer recognised.

And that was the worst ache of all.

As the hours dragged on, I couldn't take it anymore. My mind was spinning. I didn't know what had happened to Joshua. He was only two and a half. Had he woken up and found I wasn't there? Had he cried? Had he eaten? Was he still in his pyjamas? Was he walking around the house calling for me? Had anyone even noticed he was there? I felt like I was losing my mind.

I asked Patrick to call Raymond. He looked at me like he couldn't believe what I was asking. "Are you sure?" he asked.

"I don't know what else to do," I said. "My child is there. I'm pregnant. Where am I supposed to go?"

He paused, visibly uncomfortable with my decision. But he made the call anyway.

Raymond came over, full of apologies. He promised it would never happen again, swore he didn't know what had come over him. Said he'd change.

But Patrick said something that has never left me. "This is how it starts. Once a man lays his hands on a woman, it doesn't stop. This will happen again. You've been initiated—whether you know it or not—into accepting violence."

How I wish I had listened.

After that experience, we tried to rebuild our relationship, to salvage something from the wreckage. But in hindsight, I know the damage had already been done. Too many cracks had appeared, and no amount of patching could hold it all together. We sailed on for a while, trying to stay afloat, but the truth was, the water had already begun to sink the boat beyond repair. Like any sinking boat, we tried everything to keep it afloat. Temporary measures did little to stop the cracks from deepening. The arguments became more frequent, the physical fights more intense, and our disagreements outweighed our agreements. Raymond spent more time either asleep or watching television. He was distant, detached from the reality we were facing.

During this time, I was still clinging to my part-time job as a television presenter, while Raymond remained unemployed. It felt like we were barely surviving. The weight of our struggles pressed down on me, and I knew something had to change.

In desperation, I reached out to my family again. I couldn't carry the burden alone anymore. Slowly, I began to open up to my parents about the situation—but carefully, I avoided mentioning the abuse. I still wanted to protect Raymond's respect in their eyes. As always, my dependable father immediately offered his support. He began reaching out to well-placed relatives and contacts to seek employment opportunities or leads for me. While those efforts were underway, he would send money to help with food and bills. It wasn't a fortune, but it provided a much-needed sense of relief during this time.

Despite his help, the tension at home only worsened. The strain of everything—the broken trust, the emotional and physical abuse and the overall instability took its toll. I couldn't shake the feeling that we were going to sink completely.

CALEB

On April 23rd, 2009, Caleb arrived earlier than expected. During a routine ultrasound, the doctor discovered that his umbilical cord was tightly wrapped around his neck. With concern, he prepared me for an emergency C-section. By God's grace, Caleb was born healthy, weighing just over 3 kilograms. Naming him was easy—where there's a Joshua, there must be a Caleb. Raymond and I both agreed on the name without hesitation.

My mother, reflecting the significance of his birth, named him Natukunda, meaning "He loves us" in Runyankore, a reminder of God's enduring love for us. Despite the struggles we were facing, my father was still alive, and through it all, God's grace remained evident. As a final tribute to the strength I had to summon in the face of hardship, I named him Hama, meaning "be strong." This name became a symbol of the strength I had to find within myself during those painful, trying times.

The medical bills for Caleb's delivery were covered by my savings from the television job, with my father generously topping up the remainder. However, Caleb's arrival did little to ease the tension at home. The evening we were discharged from the hospital, Raymond went out drinking and returned in the early hours of the morning. My mother, who had been up feeding Caleb, opened the door to let him in. It was around 3 or 4 AM. The state of our relationship was deteriorating rapidly, and it felt as though things couldn't get worse.

Financially, we were sinking deeper. We couldn't afford the rent for our current home, and soon, we received an eviction notice. We moved into a much smaller place—barely more than a shack. The walls were worn and weathered, the roof sagging in places, and the air inside felt damp and stale. It was tucked away behind the main houses, hidden from view. The ceiling was so low that we had to duck to avoid bumping our heads with every step. The space was cramped—no proper bedrooms, just a kitchen, living area, and sleeping space all in one. The house seemed designed to squeeze as much as possible into the smallest space imaginable, offering barely enough room to breathe, let alone dream.

The conditions were far from ideal, but it was all we could afford. We were hard pressed in almost every way, yet somehow, we kept moving forward, day by day.

CONSULT CARE

By God's grace and the favour that has always been upon my life, things began to shift. Through my father's connections, Dr Diana offered me a part-time job at Consult Care—a clinic that primarily handled laboratory blood work for Iraq recruits and other medical logistics. This opportunity, along with my television hosting job, provided just enough income to help us scrape by.

I hosted the show for almost seven years. At times, it was my main source of income; at others, it became a side hustle when sporadic opportunities came my way. Despite the many challenges we faced, these roles helped keep us afloat and allowed me to provide for my family. God's provision was evident, even in the toughest seasons.

We spent most of Caleb's baby days in that shack—a place that barely offered shelter—and it was also where Joshua began his preschool journey. A lady in the neighbourhood had opened a small home-school program, and I thought it was a wonderful idea for Joshua to attend a few hours a week to help him interact with other children and prepare for school.

Amid the turbulence of that season, my father gifted me my first car, recognising how unsafe it was to travel by *boda boda* with two young children—especially in the rain. Though modest, that car was a great blessing in the chaos of those days.

Sadly, the most heartbreaking moments of my marriage unfolded within those very walls. Raymond cheated on me multiple times—not through whispers or rumours, but through his own confession. He told me everything: with whom, where, and when. He was rarely home, and when he was, he remained distant, lost in his own world, never helping with the children. My house help became my only reliable support. I leaned on her to care for Joshua and Caleb while I worked to provide for our family.

To keep things afloat, I juggled everything I could. In addition to my existing roles, I leaned into my creative side—making keychains and letter bracelets using metallic-coloured alphabet beads to spell out names or words—and sold them to friends and their friends. Each piece was handmade with care, and every sale, no matter how small, gave me a sense of hope and agency in a time that felt otherwise overwhelming.

That hope, however, often lived alongside heartbreak.

I remember the fights—physical, emotional, and financial—so clearly. They had become part of our daily existence, and the weight of it all settled heavily on my heart. The tension and chaos began to affect Joshua, too. He had just started talking, and his speech was now somewhat clear. Cognitively, he was beginning to understand more than I wished he did. Whenever his father yelled, Joshua would step in—both physically and verbally—to protect me. I can still hear his little voice crying, "Daddy… stop!" His words echo in my mind to this day. I knew then that I couldn't let this continue. The stress was unbearable, and it was clear it was taking a toll on my children.

When we moved into the shack, it wasn't just the lack of space that was a struggle—it was everything. Sisqó, our loyal German

Shepherd, had nowhere proper to stay. The house was far too cramped for humans, let alone a dog of his size. He had to stay outside, tethered to his leash at night. And then, one night, Sisqó was stolen. We later heard from someone in the area that a dog breeder had probably taken him. The news shattered us, especially the boys, who had grown so close to him. Their sadness lingered for days, and the loss of Sisqó was just one more weight on top of an already heavy chapter in our lives.

The job at Consult Care didn't last long—the clinic closed when the Iraq contract ended. But during my time there, God's favour was still evident in the people He placed in my path. One such blessing was Allen, a young lady whose kindness brought much-needed support to us. Though she earned a modest salary, she often spent her hard-earned money on groceries for my family and brought food from her own home to ensure we never went without. Seeing our situation moved her to tears, as it did many others who knew our story. Through her generosity and the support of friends, God's grace sustained us in those difficult days. As the psalmist declares:

"I have been young, and now am old; yet have I not seen the righteous forsaken, nor his seed begging bread."
—Psalm 37:25 (KJV)

With help from my brother Patrick's friend, Barbara, I got another part-time job at Baylor College of Medicine in Mulago. The timing was perfect, as my friend Evelyn also worked there. My shack home was on the way to work, and Evelyn kindly offered to give me a lift most days. It was through these little acts of kindness that I saw God's faithfulness, and I knew He was making a way for us to survive.

It was at Baylor that my path crossed with Joan's, and she would go on to become so much more than just a close friend. Joan became Caleb's godmother, the younger sister I never had, a confidant who listened when the world felt too heavy, and eventually, a business partner with whom I shared so much of my journey. Her unwavering support and love were like lifelines in a sea of uncertainty. Over the years, she became a pivotal figure in my life—offering both practical help and emotional strength. In a world where true friendship and loyalty were hard to come by, Joan became my rock, always there when I needed her most.

THE STEWARDSHIP OF PAIN

But despite all these blessings, nothing in my marriage changed. The environment remained toxic, and by the start of 2010, I had had enough. It wasn't healthy for Joshua and Caleb to keep living in such instability. I knew I had to remove myself—and the boys—from it all, to try and give them some semblance of normalcy.

I told Raymond that I was leaving. I was taking the boys and moving out—for their sake and mine. We had to find peace, somewhere, somehow.

Raymond had long since disengaged. His emotional absence was matched only by his physical unavailability at home. And when I said the words out loud—"I'm leaving, and I'm taking the children"—there was no objection. No protest. Just silence.

Maybe, deep inside, he had been waiting for this moment. Perhaps it was his silent prayer. Maybe he, too, was tired of everything but felt trapped in it all. Maybe this was the release he needed but didn't know how to ask for. I wondered: did he sigh with relief?

I was leaving. I was taking the kids. And in the African setting, a man's children—especially his boys—are everything. You can take all else, but not his children.

Not Raymond.

He did not resist.

It hurt that he didn't fight for his family or even try to stop me. But at the same time, I was glad he didn't. His silence confirmed what I had feared and tried for so long to deny—that I hadn't imagined it, that I hadn't misread the signs.

This was it.

The reality.

And now, I had to face it for what it was—not what I had hoped it could be.

I had a heart-to-heart with my brother David about the circumstances I was facing and asked for his help in rebuilding my life. He listened carefully and, with a deep understanding of the situation, agreed. He said it was better to protect the boys than to expose them to the trauma of watching the ongoing chaos in our marriage. He understood that the damage caused by such dysfunction could leave scars that would last a lifetime.

David not only offered generous financial support to help me start over, but he also provided a professional reference that spoke not to connections, but to my character, work ethic, and potential. Somehow, that opened a door I never imagined would be mine to walk through.

On 18th August 2010, I was officially appointed as a Research Officer on Special Duties in the Office of the Coordinator of Intelligence—a role within the President's Office. The title sounded grand, almost too grand for where I was in life at the time. The pay didn't quite match its formality, but that hardly mattered. His assistance marked a pivotal turning point in my life, offering not just the means to rebuild, but also the dignity of purpose.

With this part-time opportunity, I began to chart a new course for myself and my children—one that led us away from the toxicity that had stifled us for far too long. It was more than a job; it was a declaration of hope, and the beginning of a different kind of future.

You might be wondering about the sporadic nature of my employment over the years. The truth is, the job market in Uganda can be highly unpredictable. Salaries are often so low that it's nearly impossible to rely on one job alone. Many people move between short-term opportunities, hustling just to stay afloat. In a climate where wages barely cover life's essentials, it's not unusual to juggle multiple roles or pick up side gigs simply to survive.

When stability is rare, adaptability becomes essential.

There were seasons when I had to take whatever came my way—consulting, part-time roles, volunteer work, informal sales—anything that could put food on the table. It wasn't about building a conventional career ladder; it was about keeping the lights on, paying school fees, and doing whatever it took to make ends meet. This was the rhythm I came to know well—periods of hustle, followed by dry spells—all dictated by a system where reliable employment was the exception, not the norm.

REBUILD TO TEAR DOWN?

With David's unwavering support behind me, I signed the lease on a modest two-bedroom house near Bidandi Close, in Bukoto's Nsimbiziwome Village—about a ten-minute drive from St. Francis Primary School in Ntinda Kigoowa. It felt right. I was proud of this achievement. After everything we had been through, this wasn't just a better address—it was a step out of the shack, in every sense.

For the first time in a long while, I felt I was giving my boys something solid: a safe roof, a steady rhythm, and the chance to just be children. Caleb could begin pre-primary, and Joshua could continue without switching schools.

The move brought a strange mix of relief and vulnerability. I had no idea what the coming months would look like—but I knew we were no longer stuck. Then came a gift that brought unexpected joy. My beautiful niece Stella gave the boys a Maltese puppy named Spencer. From the moment he burst through the door, all fluff and energy, the house came alive.

The boys, still unsettled by the move and the absence of their father, found in Spencer a source of comfort and distraction. They took to him instantly—laughing as he chased his tail, settling when he curled up beside them at night. Spencer brought lightness into our home. He wasn't just a pet; he was proof that love could still find its way to us, even here.

It was a fresh start. Not perfect, not easy—but ours. That thought kept me steady.

As I wrapped up my part-time role at Baylor College and continued presenting on television, I stepped into my new job as a Research Officer. The title sounded more glamorous than it was—but it gave me just enough. Together, those roles offered structure, income, and a way forward. A way to rebuild not just our lives, but our sense of dignity and direction.

At the same time, I decided to dive into a more entrepreneurial path. More accurately, I became a hawker. Joan and I started selling clothes, shoes, bags, jewellery, and bedding to friends and their circles. It was a modest beginning, but it felt empowering to take control of something tangible—a steady foothold amid the shifting tides of unpredictability. The business wasn't large, but it gave me a sense of purpose and independence in a sea of challenges.

God's provision showed up through friends and acquaintances who offered help when it was needed most. We were never without. We had food, shelter, and rent. And we found a steady source of support in Kiconco, a new house help who joined us during that fragile transition.

Now, it's important to understand something about the role of house help in Uganda. Unlike in many Western settings where domestic assistance might be seen as a luxury or status symbol, in Uganda, it is a practical necessity—an integral part of how many households function. Regardless of income level, many families have someone to help care for the children, cook, clean, or manage day-to-day needs. It's less about wealth and more about balance—about building a network of mutual support in a society where extended family and community are central.

In many homes, house helps are far more than employees; they become part of the family. Children grow up calling them 'Auntie' or 'Uncle,' not out of politeness but out of genuine affection and respect. They're woven into the rhythms of everyday life—trusted with routines, responsibilities, and relationships that carry deep meaning. They celebrate milestones, shoulder burdens, and hold space in the family's emotional landscape.

For me, in this season, Kiconco was all of that and more. She brought structure to our new life, calm to the chaos, and care to the boys when I had to be out chasing work or navigating the next steps. Her presence gave me the space to breathe, and to focus on healing—for myself and for my sons. She wasn't just helping in the home; she was helping hold us together.

THE WEIGHT OF EXPECTATIONS

After some time, life began to settle. The boys and I had found a rhythm, and things were going relatively well. We had a roof over our heads, school routines in place, and a growing sense of peace. But just as calm began to take root, familiar voices from home began to echo in my ears—my parents, their friends, and members of the church community.

They began to counsel me—gently, then persistently—urging me to consider reconciling with Raymond. For the sake of marriage. For the sake of the children. For the sake of the family unit. They reminded me of the vows we had taken, the "until death do us part" promise, and the sacred covenant of keeping a family together, especially for the children's well-being.

I listened.

I acknowledged their concerns, but I also stood firm—at least at first.

Raymond, in my eyes, had already broken those vows. He had abandoned the commitment, dishonoured the trust, and shattered the foundation we were meant to build upon. Why was the burden now mine to carry?

And yet... as time passed, I softened.

I found myself praying for reconciliation. I didn't take the idea lightly. It was something I wrestled with—something that lived in my private prayers and long silences. The shame of a broken marriage weighs heavily in any society, but it carries an especially sharp sting in African culture. Marriage is not just a union between two people; it's a community expectation, a family statement, a social contract.

I entered into deep moments of reflection and prayer—questioning, weeping, and asking God to guide my heart.

Could something so broken be mended?

Was it pride in what I had now built that was keeping me away—or was it wisdom?

Then, one morning, Raymond showed up uninvited.

The sky hung low, heavy with clouds that hadn't yet made up their mind. The kind of morning that felt unsure of itself—much like me. The boys were at school. He must have known that. Or maybe he didn't care.

There he was. No call. No warning. No gift in hand—not even a sweet for the boys. He said he'd come to see them, but they weren't home. So what now?

He stood at the door, awkward but familiar. There was no drama in his eyes, just a quiet hope he tried to mask with casual talk. I had seen that look before—years ago, in better times. His eyes lit up when I mentioned the idea of reconciliation, though he quickly buried it under a shrug and stories of how well he was doing on his own. He'd heard I was doing well too.

My voice trembled when I spoke. I hadn't planned to bring it up, but something inside me reached for that thread of possibility.

It wasn't easy. It wasn't clear.

But it felt... necessary.

Or was it?

Even as I let him inside—both the house and the conversation—I wasn't sure what I was inviting. Was this healing? Or history repeating itself in softer tones?

Hope and doubt now walked with me, step for step.

His visits became more frequent. He started dropping by often, staying longer each time.

Oddly, almost always when the boys weren't home.

That made me wonder. Was he ashamed? Was he easing his way back in, or just avoiding the full weight of what it meant to be a father again? I couldn't tell.

Then one day, in the middle of a slow afternoon, he asked if he could move back in.

Huh!

That was the only word I had in that moment. A sound, not a sentence.

Because what do you say when the past knocks twice?

The question caught me off guard.

Fear gripped me, not of him, but of what this would mean.

How would I explain this to my brother David—the one who had helped me rebuild my life, pulled me from the wreckage, and given me a fresh start?

And what about my friends, the ones who had surrounded me like a safety net during my darkest days?

And Kiconco, who had loved and cared for the boys as if they were her own?

They had brought groceries, fuel, clothes, emotional support, done school pickups, and even planned a surprise birthday dinner just to lift my spirits.

They had carried me. And now I was—what? Inviting chaos back in?

But the voices of 'reason' were louder than my fear. The ever-present hum of cultural expectation, family pressure, and my desire to believe in redemption... wore me down.

So, I said yes. I allowed it.

Raymond left the bar he had been both running and living at and came to live with us.

And for a brief, flickering moment, I believed this might be a fresh start. A chance to rebuild our lives. A new chapter.

But I was wrong. So very wrong.

It quickly became clear that we weren't starting over—we were resuming the dysfunction, only now with new characters and greater intensity.

Within weeks, Raymond had reverted to his old ways—and worse.

He had expanded his social circle through the bar scene and was more connected than ever to people whose presence brought nothing but destruction.

He resumed his late-night activities, often staying out until dawn and returning home in the early morning.

And as soon as he drifted into sleep, his phone would begin vibrating—messages from women, one after another. I saw them. I knew what they meant.

The betrayal was no longer hidden. It was blatant. Bold.

I remember one instance vividly. Joan and I had travelled to China for business.

Before I left, I reminded Raymond about Joshua's school pick-up schedule.

He assured me, confidently, that he would handle it.

He promised.

While on a layover in Ethiopia, I decided to call Kiconco to check on how things were going at home and see how the boys were managing in my absence. I expected a routine update, maybe a few words of reassurance. But as soon as she picked up, I could hear the tremble in her voice.

"*Taata* Joshua is not back... Joshua is not here. I don't know what to do."

My heart dropped.

It was already well past school hours—too late to contact the school or make any alternative arrangements. I was thousands of kilometres away, helpless, caught between countries, between time zones, between a mother's instinct to protect and the limitations of distance.

All I could do was make a desperate prayer for my child's safety—pleading silently that he was somewhere warm, fed, and unharmed. I hoped the boarding section at school had made some overnight arrangements for him, perhaps giving him a bed, something to eat, and a place to wait out the night. Or maybe—though I dreaded the thought—his father had picked him up and was gallivanting with him somewhere, thoughtlessly dragging him along into God-knows-what kind of night. The not knowing was agony. There was nothing more I could do but wait for the morning, when Kiconco would drop Caleb off at school and, God willing, get some answers about where Joshua had spent the night.

When morning finally came, so did the explanation.

Joshua had spent the night with the boarding students.

Raymond—his father—had gone out drinking and simply forgotten to pick him up.

When I confronted him, shaken and horrified, his response was chilling in its flatness:

"I forgot."

That was it.

I was stunned. You forgot?

Your child?

Not a chore, not an errand. Your son.

How could anyone forget something so basic, yet so deeply significant? How could a father not grasp the weight of that kind of neglect—the fear, the danger, the abandonment?

That moment, like so many others, spoke volumes about where we truly stood—not just as partners, but as co-parents, and as a family.

And once again, the silence between us was louder than anything he could have said.

You would think that by this point, I would have realised things weren't just failing—they were collapsing.

The progress and stability we had managed to build during our separation was disintegrating, piece by piece, replaced by confusion and emotional chaos.

But no.

I held on to hope. I clung to the idea that perhaps Raymond was simply struggling to adjust. That maybe this return, this second chance, required more patience. More time. More grace. And as a Christian woman, shouldn't I be the one to extend it?

I told myself I could be better.

More submissive. More understanding. More faithful.

And so, I tried.

I extended grace again.

I forgave him again.

I made excuses for his behaviour, convincing myself that love was patient, love was kind, and love endured all things.

I thought, maybe if I showed unwavering support. Maybe if I give him all my paychecks. Maybe then things will change.

So, I did exactly that.

In my desperation to salvage what little semblance of a marriage we had left, I surrendered my financial independence, handing over every cent I earned. I hoped it would create a sense of shared responsibility. A foundation. A reason to rebuild.

But it didn't.

The money vanished.

It wasn't used to support the household or care for the children. Instead, it went toward himself—fancy shoes, limited edition Nike sneakers, and other personal indulgences.

Meanwhile, we lacked the most basic necessities.

And whenever I brought up the issue of provision, of responsibility, of fairness—it was like lighting a fuse.

Arguments erupted.

Shouting matches followed.

Sometimes, those arguments turned physical.

It didn't matter how hard I tried.

My sacrifices seemed to mean nothing.

The more I gave, the more I realised something painful:

I was fighting to save a marriage he had no intention of fighting for.

One evening, an argument—its details now blurred by time and trauma—escalated beyond anything I could have imagined. In a sudden, terrifying moment, Joshua stepped in to mediate, to protect. I watched in helpless horror as Raymond lifted him and hurled him into the bunk bed. Joshua's head struck the wooden frame with a sickening thud, and his leg tore open on impact. Blood flowed freely from the gash, a wound so deep it left a scar he carries to this day—a permanent mark of a night he has never forgotten, one he has recounted many times since.

That scar on Joshua's leg felt like an imprint of the wounds carved silently into my spirit. And yet, I stayed. I hoped. I prayed.

I rationalised. I made excuses. But deep within me, the truth was starting to press harder against my denial: this wasn't mere dysfunction—this was destruction.

Still, to the outside world, we seemed... fine. Polished. Put together. We had perfected the art of the performance, presenting ourselves as the picture of a loving, united couple. At events, we smiled. We laughed. He held my hand like any proud husband would. Whenever he had the microphone—especially if he was MCing—he'd speak of his "gorgeous wife, N*unu*," lavishing praise and affection in a voice everyone could hear. He would recount, with impressive flair, the sacrifices I'd made for our family, painting me as the quiet hero behind our success.

The audience adored it. Some of my friends, who knew the truth behind the façade, would nod along and smile gently, careful not to provoke discomfort or risk his displeasure. They understood the delicate dance we had to perform in public. They played their part because they knew—just as I did—that this curated image was far from our reality.

You might be thinking, Surely this man must have done some good? One can't be all bad. And yes, you'd be right. He was funny—charming, even—with a sharp sense of humour that could light up a room. There were moments when he did do good things, and when he was kind, it felt genuine. But those moments never lasted. They were like flickers of light—brief and bright—but always swallowed again by the dark.

Isn't it strange how the weight of the bad can so easily eclipse the good? It's as if the human heart, in its vulnerability, clings more tightly to pain. The sweetness of brighter moments fades quickly, slipping into the background like a forgotten melody, while the wounds linger, sharp and persistent.

Still, I do recall glimpses of happiness. There were times when we'd go out as a family—movie nights, dinners at modest restaurants. Fleeting, quiet joys that, for a little while, disguised the strain beneath the surface. But even in those moments, my mind never fully rested. I was always calculating, always anxious—thinking of what we lacked at home. Each outing felt like a luxury we couldn't afford, a temporary indulgence that came at too high a cost. Raymond, however, was drawn to the idea of the "good life"—to appearances, to enjoyment, to a version of success that always seemed just out of reach.

I should mention something significant about his time in Iraq. While working there, Raymond built connections with some of the Americans he worked alongside. One of them, a man named Don, introduced him to a Christian adoption agency in the United States. The agency was looking for local contacts in Uganda to help facilitate international adoptions. Raymond stepped into that role with ease. He became a liaison of sorts—guiding adoptive parents through the process, hosting them during their stay, driving them to appointments with lawyers and baby homes, and sometimes even organising short cultural excursions to help them experience the country.

The work was seasonal—intense during certain months, quiet in others—but it paid well. Raymond would sometimes share the details with me: how much a family paid, how long they stayed, what services he'd provided. But his transparency ended there. If I later asked for money—even for essentials—it would often spiral into conflict. He'd become defensive, hostile even, and the atmosphere in the house would shift instantly.

Over time, I stopped asking.

I stayed in my lane, quietly managing household expenses, stretching what I had, and making do in silence. I kept my financial matters to myself. It wasn't ideal—not even close—but it allowed for a brittle kind of peace. A fragile illusion of harmony that kept the storms at bay, at least for a little while. My silence became my shield, a quiet form of self-preservation in a home where conflict was always waiting to erupt.

CANAAN

My father's health continued to decline, necessitating frequent trips to Kampala for medical attention. Just before Canaan was born, David proposed a practical and generous solution: we needed a bigger house where my parents could have their room and privacy during these visits. He even offered to contribute up to one million Ugandan shillings toward the rent. After discussing this with Raymond, we both saw it as a blessing. If we could find a house that cost no more than David's contribution, we wouldn't need to pay anything for rent ourselves.

With this plan in mind, I reached out to a house broker, and within days, he had found a promising option. One viewing was all it took—I knew instantly: this was the one. Located in Kulambiro, the house stood tall and gleaming—a brand-new, double-storey with three ensuite bedrooms. Every part of it felt spacious and thoughtfully designed. The lounge was wide and bright, the kitchen crisp and modern, with enough room to move freely—such a contrast from what we had known. The balconies opened to fresh air and gentle views, and the yard offered enough space for the boys to play. The gated community brought with it a rare sense of quiet and safety.

When we first moved in, our few belongings looked small in those large rooms—but I didn't mind. I had saved up enough to start fresh, and I was finally in a place where I could choose things that matched the dignity of our new home. I bought curtains that softened the sunlight and kitchenware that fit the space.

I was beyond delighted. Content

By now, we find ourselves in 2012. We've journeyed through quite a bit, haven't we? I hope I haven't worn you out. Stick with me—it's like they say: if you want to go fast, go alone; if you want to go far, go together. Is that how it goes? Who even came up with that? Anyway, let's press on.

Saturday, 1 December 2012. Early morning. Another precious soul joined the world—a beautiful, bouncing baby boy named Canaan. And when I say "bouncing," I mean it. This kid tipped the scales at 5 kilos! I reckon my body had been prepped and primed by the twin pregnancy and Caleb before him, so Canaan had plenty of room to grow. Spacious quarters, you might say.

Now, you're probably raising an eyebrow or two, thinking? Another baby? After all the challenges she just told us about—marriage on the brink, unresolved chaos—what was she thinking? Let me answer that for you: I thought, maybe a daughter would balance things out. Two boys and a girl, right? A nice, harmonious dynamic. At the time, I don't think I was consciously planning it that way, but deep down, perhaps I was longing for a daughter to fill the void left by the one I'd lost.

I remember going for the ultrasound. I was so eager to find out the gender, heart quietly hoping for it to be a girl. When the sonographer announced, "It's a boy," I cried. And not just a quiet sniffle, mind you—full-on sobbing. I sat up and blurted, "Oh no… why? Another boy?" Was it hormones? Disappointment? Maybe a mix of both. Oh well. Either way, he was destined to be Canaan.

And let me tell you, Canaan was perfect. The most beautiful baby I'd ever laid eyes on to this day. Biased? Maybe. But everyone said the same thing—he was adorable, an absolute masterpiece. And to top it off, his birth went smoothly, free of complications. I had agreed to have half anaesthesia during the caesarean, which meant I was fully awake and could watch the doctors at work. For those unfamiliar, this is how it works: with a spinal anaesthetic or epidural, only the lower half of your body is numbed, leaving you conscious but without any sensation in the area being operated on.

It's surreal, really—there you are, lying on the operating table, wide awake, while a whole team of professionals is busy delivering your baby. You can feel the pressure and tugging, but no pain. It's like watching the most bizarre reality TV show ever, except you're the star, the plot revolves around your uterus, and the grand prize is your baby.

I remember trying to process it all, my mind racing through a marathon of thoughts. On one hand, I was in awe of the medical marvel unfolding right before my (metaphorical) eyes. On the other, I couldn't help but marvel at the sheer weirdness of it all. It's not every day you find yourself wide awake while someone is quite literally pulling a new human out of your abdomen. The sensation was surreal, almost like watching a science fiction movie, except I was the one in the scene.

Life loves a bit of drama, doesn't it? Or maybe it's just my life. Honestly, sometimes I wonder. Shortly after Canaan's arrival, malaria came knocking—except it didn't knock, it barged in, uninvited and relentless. Feverish and trapped in my bed, it left me bedridden for weeks. There were moments when I was so delirious I thought I might be at death's door, standing there, waiting patiently for someone to open it and let me in. But somehow, through sheer will (and probably a lot of prayer), I muddled through.

It was a season of reflection—a time to pause and take stock of the journey I had walked so far. Despite the chaos of the past few months, a deep sense of gratitude settled within me. Both my parents were alive, present, and ready to help in every way possible. In the midst of all that uncertainty and turmoil, their support was a constant—like a safe harbour in a storm.

This, I realised, is what every mother craves, isn't it? To be reminded that no matter how grown you are, no matter how many children of your own you have, you are still someone's child. Always. There's a deep comfort in that, a quiet assurance that no matter how turbulent the waters of life become, there's always someone who sees you, holds you, and reminds you that you matter.

My parents, bless their hearts, showered me with the kind of love and care that only parents can give. I felt so nurtured, so protected, that I slept in their room during my recovery from malaria and childbirth. Here I was, a mother of three, and yet, to them, I was still their precious baby girl. My dad, 87, and my mum, 73, were both dealing with their health challenges, but they never hesitated to pour themselves into my care. I was beyond grateful to have them—not just alive, but with me.

As I held baby Canaan in my arms, I thought to myself, this is it. Baby number three. The end of that chapter. I knew there would be no more pregnancies, not unless I fancied gambling for another boy in my dream of having a daughter.

Now, knowing the financial strain my previous births had caused, I had tried to be clever this time. I'd diligently stashed away my LTV pay to cover medical expenses—doctor's fees, the C-section, medication, hospital bills... you name it. And let me tell you, in Uganda, where Medicare is but a foreign concept, this was no small feat.

But, as life loves to remind me, plans often go astray. My savings didn't stretch far enough. Enter Raymond. For once, he stepped up and covered the remaining costs. For a fleeting, glorious moment, I allowed myself to exhale. Relief swept over me like a warm breeze.

And then, because life has the comedic timing of a slapstick movie, I discovered that Raymond had stolen all the money I'd earned selling stock out of my car boot. Yep. My hard-earned cash, meant to replenish stock for the business I was managing, was gone.

What was I supposed to tell Joan, my business partner, who was studying in Korea and had entrusted me with the business? Would she even believe me if I explained what had happened? And here's the kicker—Raymond didn't even own up. Nope, not at first. He sent me on a wild goose chase instead.

Naturally, I thought the maid had done it. She hadn't been with us long—just a temporary replacement while Kiconco, who had been part of our family for years, was away visiting her relatives. I'd hired her urgently, knowing I would soon be in hospital to deliver Canaan and needed someone to help care for the boys and my father in my absence.

Raymond had planted the seed, and I—consumed with anger and overwhelmed by everything pressing in—let it grow. I confronted the poor woman, and let's just say, things escalated quickly. Her responses were contradictory and confusing— "Yes, I took it… no, I didn't…"—every unsure word fuelling the fire already raging in me. I became someone I barely recognised, driven more by frustration and fatigue than reason. I was a woman stretched too thin, and at that moment, I broke.

The situation spiralled out of control. In the midst of the shouting, the pacing, the fury—I somehow ended up with a deep cut under my foot. It didn't heal properly. The wound got infected, and later, a doctor told me I had been dangerously close to developing gangrene. To this day, that cut left behind more than just a scar—it became a symbolic reminder of that incident. A deep tissue wound that still flares up occasionally, especially if I dare wear heels for too long. Let's just say Stilettos and I parted ways permanently after that. These days, it's flats and block heels only—comfort over fashion, every time.

And then, a year later—an entire year—Raymond finally admitted he was the culprit. A whole twelve months of my anger, my confusion, my guilt over how I'd treated that woman. When he finally came clean, I didn't know whether to laugh, cry, or scream. Maybe I did all three.

That was a new low—even for Raymond.

David and I often discussed family matters at his office. One evening, after work, he gave me advice that has stayed with me. "If you divorce, it will destroy our father," he told me. "He is old and unwell, as you can see. Hold on, fight on. If it's finances, I will do my best to help you out. Talk to Juliet; she will help you. But whatever you do, try to keep it together for the parents' sake." His words carried the weight of responsibility and the importance of family unity. He reminded me how rare divorce was in our family. Only one of my older siblings, Damalie, had been divorced, and even then, she lived in the UK, far removed from the local environment. Here, I would be the only one divorced, carrying the stigma, and shaming our parents, especially with my father's fragile health.

Juliet, David's wife, stepped in to support me in ways that relieved many of my burdens. She helped with rent and school fees for the boys.

As always, my tribe of friends became an incredible source of strength during this season—just as they had been over the years. To mention but a few: Joan, Norah, Evelyn, Fifi, Mimi, Alice, Cathy, Allen, Doreen K., Doris, Immy, Dr Doreen (our dentist), my cousins Esther and Sarah M., and my nieces Stella, Hope, and Sharon all stood by me. Each one contributed in their unique way—whether by buying items from me to support my business, offering business loans, shopping for clothes for the boys, giving me clothes of their own, or simply being there to listen. Their kindness and generosity were beyond measure, and I often wonder how I can ever repay them. I hope they know how much they mean to me, as I've tried to express my gratitude to each of them.

To ease transportation—especially for taking my father to his medical appointments—David bought me a white Toyota Vista Ardeo. It was a significant upgrade from my old Starlet, both in comfort and in image. In Uganda, cars are a symbol of status, and this one felt undeniably luxurious. David didn't mince words—he said my Starlet was "not only embarrassing but unacceptable for driving his father."

Fair enough, I thought. And truthfully, I was proud. Sliding into that car for the first time felt like stepping into a new season—one where dignity and ease could finally coexist. It wasn't just about appearances; it was about honouring my father with the best.

However, my joy was short-lived. Within three weeks, Raymond started using the car occasionally. Then, one day, he declared that the car was "dead" and that the mechanic had advised it was beyond repair and unsafe to drive. He arranged for its sale, but I never saw the proceeds. I was left without a car. When my father came to Kampala, eager to see the vehicle I had told him about, I had to explain its mysterious demise. He was shocked by the story and confronted Raymond, eventually concluding that Raymond's ego had been bruised by my excitement over David's gift. My mother stepped in and topped up the funds for me to buy a blue three-door Rav4—a car I absolutely loved. It was a reminder of my family's enduring love and support.

EVERYTHING, EVERYWHERE, ALL AT ONCE

On April 29, 2013, David authored a letter to Brigadier Ronald Balya, the Director General of the Internal Security Organisation (ISO). In this letter, he called for an investigation into allegations of a plot to eliminate high-ranking government officials who were opposed to what he referred to as the "Muhoozi Project"—a purported plan to position President Museveni's son, Brigadier Muhoozi Kainerugaba, as his successor. David's letter specifically urged the ISO to investigate claims that senior officials, including himself, Prime Minister Amama Mbabazi, and Chief of Defence Forces General Aronda Nyakairima, were being targeted due to their perceived opposition to this succession plan. He also raised concerns about the possibility of stage-managed attacks, such as the one on Mbuya barracks in March 2013, being used to frame these officials. The publication of this letter on May 7, 2013, sent shockwaves through Uganda, igniting a political storm that would alter the course of many lives—including mine. At the time, David was away on official duty, scheduled to return on May 11. But he never did. An arrest warrant had been issued in anticipation of his arrival, leaving him with no choice but to seek asylum in London, citing grave threats to his safety.

The Ugandan government wasted no time in its response. Media houses that had dared to report on the letter were raided, their operations crippled under state pressure. But the crackdown didn't stop there. David's office—our office—was swiftly disbanded. Just like that, our jobs were gone, and our careers were wiped out in an instant. Some of my colleagues were not as fortunate as I was; they were arrested, detained without clear charges, and swallowed by a system that thrived on fear and silence.

As the news reports spread, a knot of dread tightened in my stomach. Every mention of David was like a dagger—twisting deeper, reopening wounds I hadn't yet learned to close. The safety we once knew had vanished, and in its place was fear, loud and lingering. I would sit quietly, the room thick with tension, the weight of the world pressing down on my shoulders as I wondered how I could protect my children from a fear that had already seeped into the corners of our home.

The uncertainty was suffocating. Our family bore the weight of relentless scrutiny, with David's name tied to daily headlines—each report tightening the noose around us all. Enemies of the state, we had become. Friends disappeared. Alliances crumbled. We were left navigating a landscape where trust had become a luxury we could no longer afford. Every decision, every whispered conversation, every cautious move we made was shaped by the constant undercurrent of tension. We were always bracing—never breathing fully—living as if under siege in our own lives.

Then, in November 2013, tragedy struck.

My brother Daniel drowned in a dam on our farm under mysterious circumstances. The news came like a punch to the gut—sudden, breathless, brutal. There was an investigation, yes, but its outcome offered no comfort. Just vague conclusions, a blur of paperwork, and more questions than answers.

Was it an accident linked to his long-standing mental health struggles, or was there something darker beneath the surface? We'll never know. The investigation left us empty-handed and hollow-hearted, crippled by fear and haunted by grief that refused to settle.

Losing Daniel was a wound we could not heal. With David in exile, our family's foundation cracked further under the strain. The pressure from every direction—political, personal, emotional—became a burden I felt ill-equipped to bear.

I couldn't afford to sit still while life continued to fall apart around me. Desperate for a way out, I turned to Norah—a well-travelled, highly connected, and deeply informed friend. I needed guidance and a plan. Leaving the country felt like the only option—a leap into the unknown that was both terrifying and necessary. I had to regain some sense of control, even if it meant stepping into the shadows.

ANCHORS OF HOPE

Norah had a way of moving through life like she was always ten steps ahead. Quick-thinking, deeply connected, and endlessly resourceful—she didn't just offer help; she delivered solutions with astonishing speed. Her efficiency was remarkable, almost uncanny, as though she could see around corners while the rest of us were still figuring out where to begin. It was one of the things I admired most about her—her ability to act swiftly and decisively, especially when everything around me felt uncertain. So, when she reached out to Alex on my behalf, I felt an immediate surge of gratitude. He was someone I had heard about but never met. What began as a simple introduction soon unfolded into a meaningful friendship. Alex had a way of seeing strength in me that I hadn't yet recognised in myself. Amid the upheaval of my life, his calm belief became a quiet source of courage. With every conversation, we began to map out a way forward, and I started to feel the threads of a new life taking shape. Norah's presence remained constant—driving things forward, reminding me that I wasn't alone, and showing me, through her actions, that hope could be practical as well as emotional. Together, we began to sketch out a future—not without fear, but no longer without direction.

Alex became a crucial part of my journey as I started to find my way forward. At first, I was convinced that Canada would be my sanctuary, the place where I could piece my life back together. But Alex had a different vision. He wholeheartedly believed that Australia was the better option. To help sway me, he introduced me to his brother, Joseph.

Joseph spoke about Australia with such enthusiasm and passion that it was hard not to get swept up in it. As he shared stories of its vibrant culture and stunning landscapes, my long-held dreams of Canada started to fade away. It felt like a light bulb moment—suddenly, my heart knew that Australia was where I needed to be.

Feeling a mix of excitement and nervous anticipation, I gathered all the necessary documents and put together my application. I managed to submit everything before the end of November, and it felt like I was truly stepping into a new chapter of my life. The thought of the change ahead was both thrilling and a little scary, but for the first time in a long while, I felt a spark of hope.

While I waited for the outcome, I began preparing—financially, mentally and emotionally. I thought through what life in Australia would look like for me and the children. Even Raymond, hesitant at first, was on board this time. Perhaps desperation had softened his stance, or maybe he too saw that we were headed nowhere fast. With no job prospects—now that my family and all its extensions were labelled government enemies—and the whisper of David's betrayal tainting every social circle we had once belonged to, there was nothing left for us here.

Then came the rejection. The visa denial was a crushing blow. All the hope I had carefully nurtured, all the plans I had begun to shape, collapsed in an instant. But perhaps it's in my nature—I did not stay down for long. Instead, the rejection fuelled a new resolve in me. If one door had closed, I would find another way. Determined,

I threw myself into research, combing through the internet daily for any international events in Australia—conferences, workshops, summits—anything that could be a doorway to a new life. If one attempt had failed, then I would make another. And another. Because a single rejection would not define my future. Not yet.

But for a moment, I stepped away from the frantic search, forcing myself to pause and see what remained. To acknowledge what God had already done. I was here. My children were healthy. We had survived. That had to count for something.

Time moved swiftly, indifferent to the weight of our struggles. Soon, December 1st arrived, and it was Canaan's first birthday. A milestone filled with joy, yet shadowed by so much. David was gone. The steady support we had once relied on had been severed, and the ground beneath us felt increasingly unstable, like sinking sand. I had already left my job at the TV station, choosing to dedicate myself fully to the research work—which now no longer existed. Yet life pressed forward, demanding we do the same. So we did, finding strength in what little we had, holding on to hope even when the future felt like a question with no clear answer.

As always, my friends rallied around, lifting the weight off my shoulders, if only for a day. They helped me put together a grand feast, filling our home with the comforting sounds of children laughing and old friends reconnecting. Those I hadn't seen in a while extended their sympathies—not just for the loss of Daniel, but in a way, for the loss of David too.

And then, December 23rd—the day I turned 30.

Raymond, surprisingly, took the lead and organised a celebration at home. I remember the music drifting softly through the room, the low hum of conversation, and the flickering candlelight casting gentle shadows against the night. For a fleeting moment, the weight on my chest lifted. I allowed the laughter to wrap around me like a fragile embrace, and for the first time in a long while, I let the joy of others seep into my weary bones. It didn't erase the pain, but it paused it. It gave me breath.

And then Christmas 2013 came.

But I remember almost nothing of it. It passed in a blur—like a dream I couldn't quite wake from—lost in the haze of exhaustion, disorientation, and unspoken grief. A holiday meant for joy, reflection, and warmth arrived like a stranger at my door. I went through the motions, but nothing touched me. The lights felt dimmer, the songs quieter, the celebration hollow. All I could feel was the heaviness of a life that no longer fit—like wearing someone else's skin. A future I had once clung to now felt like it was dissolving, slipping further and further out of reach.

Still, I wasn't ready to surrender.

While the world celebrated and rested, I returned to searching. To hoping. To believe that somewhere beyond this moment— beyond the heartbreak, beyond the silence—a door would open. That somehow, God was still writing the next page, even if I couldn't yet read it.

A STORM NAMED 2014

The first two months of that year slipped by almost unnoticed, like a calm before a relentless tempest—unremarkable compared to the upheaval that was about to unfold. On 21 March, Joan and I travelled to China, a trip fuelled by ambition and necessity. The car trunk business had grown, and now we were ready to expand—this time into bridal wear and accessories.

Joan had recently finished her studies in Korea and was back home. Seeing that I had no steady job, she worried about me and suggested, "Let's go into full-time business." She would bring in the clients, and I would manage the shop. It made sense. As a procurement officer at the Ministry of Finance, Joan moved within a network of professionals, future brides, and well-connected clients. Her reach extended across different social circles, giving our new venture a strong foundation.

The trip was meant to be routine and unremarkable. Then came the call.

The call came from Justine. Her voice was steady, but the weight of her words cut through the distance like a blade: Raymond had packed up all his belongings and left. Even the family television was gone.

Joshua and Caleb, just seven and four at the time, were devastated. Not by their father's absence—they were too young to grasp its finality—but by the missing TV. At that age, heartbreak is measured in cartoons lost, silent living rooms, and the absence of something that once filled the air with colour and sound.

At least he hadn't forgotten to pick the children from school this time. Progress, I suppose. A far cry from that earlier debacle when Joshua had been forgotten—left to stand in his little uniform like a misplaced parcel at the school gate, eventually spending the night in the boarding section.

This, however, was not a case of temporary amnesia. No. This was a curated exit. The kind of departure that involved boxes, deliberate silence, and a clean getaway—complete with the family television, as if to say, *"I'm taking the last word, and it comes with a remote control."*

Once again, he had chosen himself—not the children, not the family. And strangely, that comforted me. They were mine. Entirely, fully, undeniably mine. I couldn't help but wonder how much worse the call would have been if he'd taken them too. I was grateful. All was not lost. In fact, all was not lost. He had made it easier for me—not just to let go, but to shed the guilt of leaving, or even asking to. At least I had tried. And now, perhaps, all the so-called voices of reason would finally see it for what it truly was.

I returned home earlier than planned, stepping into a house heavy with silence, the air thick with unspoken fears. My children's faces—sad, confused, yet relieved—were the first to greet me. They didn't fully understand what had happened or what was unfolding, but they knew enough to sense that our world was shifting beneath us. And in that moment, seeing me back was all the reassurance they needed. There was no time to grieve, no space to unravel. Survival mode took over once again. I called my friends and told them to take whatever they needed—clothes, furniture, pieces of a home I could no longer hold onto. One by one, familiar belongings disappeared, carried away in the hands of people I trusted. Watching my home dismantled like that again was devastating. And yet, strangely, there was a sense of liberation in it, too. Hearing about our situation, my cousin Esther came to my rescue. She reached out to her maternal aunt, Rose, who had just completed a set of rental houses. Unlike most landlords who demanded six months' rent upfront—an amount I simply couldn't afford—Aunt Rose understood my situation. Without hesitation, she opened her doors to us, allowing me to move in without the crushing financial pressure.

And so, we moved… again. To find our footing once more. To begin again. You're probably wondering how many times we had to move. Me too. But somehow, it always became inevitable. It was as if every time we tried to plant roots, Raymond came along with a shovel—mistaking our stability for weeds and yanking us out just as we'd begun to bloom. Still, by God's grace, we were sustained. "When thou passest through the waters, I will be with thee; and through the rivers, they shall not overflow thee" (Isaiah 43:2, KJV). And so, we picked up what was left of our peace and pressed forward. Again.

God had already placed a pillar of support in my life—Justine. When Kiconco left for her annual leave and never came back—a fate all too common and quietly accepted in many Ugandan households—I was suddenly left alone to care for a baby and two young boys, overwhelmed by the needs that stretched beyond what I could manage on my own. Then Justine arrived.

She arrived quietly, with little fuss, but from the very beginning, there was something different about her. Though she joined us in the role of a house help, she quickly became so much more. A confidant. A quiet source of strength. A calming presence when everything around me felt unsteady. In a country where domestic workers rarely stay long—often passing through on their way to new dreams or better prospects—Justine stayed.

She stayed through the noise and the silence, through the moves and the meltdowns, through the days I could barely lift my head from the weight of it all. She showed up not just for the chores, but for the hard conversations, the broken routines, and the invisible emotional labour of raising boys through chaos. To this day, I hesitate to call her a house help—because she became family. She is family.

With the move came inevitable changes, each one forcing me to navigate yet another difficult season of my life. Stability became an illusion—something I clung to for the sake of my sons, who, despite everything, were still attending the same school. But beneath the surface, our reality was shifting, and the weight of our circumstances pressed down heavily.

The bridal shop had yet to gain traction, leaving me without a steady income. Job prospects were non-existent. With my brother now labelled a government enemy, no one wanted to be seen offering help, let alone hiring me. Doors that had once been open were now firmly shut, and the isolation was palpable.

With each passing day, it became clearer that life wasn't going to just hand me a way out, I would have to take a leap of faith and carve one myself. So, I bit my lip, silenced my fears, and made a bold move to reapply for a visa to Australia on 15th April 2014.

The process required me to travel to Nairobi, Kenya, for biometrics—a journey I had never made before. Though this was my second visa application, the first had been submitted too late for me to be advised on biometric requirements. At the time, Uganda had no Australian biometric collection centre, leaving me with no choice but to venture into the unfamiliar.

I had no contacts in Nairobi and no idea where to begin. Desperation had pushed me to reach out to friends, asking if anyone knew someone who could help. That's how I was connected to Beatrice—an acquaintance of a friend, a stranger at the time, but one who would soon become a sister. With nothing but faith and determination, I boarded the night bus to Nairobi, arriving early in the morning, exhausted but resolute.

Beatrice welcomed me with open arms, as though we had known each other forever. In a city that felt vast and overwhelming, she became my guide, helping me navigate the unknown. She helped me locate the Australian Embassy offices, where I completed my biometrics. Afterwards, we shared lunch, a quiet moment of warmth in the middle of uncertainty. By nightfall, I was back on the bus, heading home, my heart heavy with hope and exhaustion.

Then, on April 24, 2014, another devastating blow struck—my older sister, Kezia, passed away.

She was many things to many people—a pillar of strength, a voice of wisdom, a woman of deep conviction. As the women's counsellor for Sembabule District, a member of the Women's Democratic Wing of Mawogola County, and a secretary at the District Service Board, she dedicated her life to service, advocating for those who had no voice. Alongside her husband, George, they were pioneer educators, shaping lives and leaving an indelible mark on their community. Her loss was more than personal; it stretched beyond our family, reaching into the very fabric of the community she had poured herself into for many years.

Yet even in death, her legacy could not shield her from the political stigma that enveloped our family. Once allies, politicians who had worked closely with her now deliberately distanced themselves, shunning her burial for fear of being perceived as sympathetic to the so-called enemies of the state. This stark reality served as a painful reminder of the steep price of losing favour—a cost that extended far beyond the grave.

LOSS, GRIEF AND UNCERTAINTY

With each passing day, the weight of everything grew heavier. My father's once indomitable spirit was now worn down by the relentless tragedies that had befallen his children. At 89, he had endured more than most, but witnessing the death of his children and the exile of others was a grief no parent should ever bear. And then there was me—now a single mother in Kampala, barely scraping by, relying on the kindness of friends to keep going. What was going to happen next? How much more could I take?

The weight of grief was immense, yet life, relentless as ever, refused to pause or stand still. Amid heartbreak, I had to keep moving forward, carrying both sorrow and the fragile hope of a new beginning.

On May 5th, 2014, I was seated at Belle Marie, absentmindedly scrolling through my phone, lost in the usual haze of waiting for brides to be. Then—a ping! An email notification popped up. I hesitated. I wasn't sure what to expect, but the moment I saw where it was from, my pulse quickened. Nothing can stop the heart from racing, whether in anticipation of good news or bracing for the worst. My chest tightened; my breath caught. I felt as if my heart might explode right out of me.

With trembling hands, I opened the email.

The visa had been granted!!!!

For the first time in what felt like forever, hope wasn't just a fragile idea—it was real, tangible, alive. A door had swung open, and before me lay a path I had only dreamed of. I didn't know what awaited me on the other side, but one thing was certain—this was my chance. My fresh start. My way forward.

I believed with all my heart that this was God's divine intervention. A providential path laid before me when I had run out of options. Gratitude filled my heart, but so did the weight of everything this decision meant. Leaving for Australia wasn't going to be just about me—it meant parting with my children, entrusting them to Justine, who had become more than just a caretaker but a second mother to them. It meant saying goodbye to my ageing parents, knowing full well that I might never see my father again. It meant stepping into the unknown with no clear timeline for when—if ever—I would be able to reunite with my boys.

I was set to leave in July, which meant I had mere weeks to prepare. There was so much to do, and so many loose ends to tie up. Canaan needed to be baptized. I had to figure out how to support Justine while I was away, sell my car to afford the plane ticket, and make countless other arrangements to ensure that life would go on for those I was leaving behind.

But just as I was in the final stages of preparing for this life-altering step, yet another tragedy struck.

On June 22, 2014, Sayuni, died. Another devastating blow. It felt as though the storms would never cease, as though each fresh loss was determined to test the limits of my endurance. How much more could my heart bear before it shattered completely?

The murmurs began. Whispers in hushed tones. Sideways glances. What had become of this home? Three siblings gone in such a short span of time. People spoke in cautious speculation, as if an explanation might somehow make sense of the strange and sorrowful turn our family had taken. But there was no explanation. Just the silence that grief brings and the heaviness that exhaustion leaves behind.

Through it all, my father stood unwavering. His faith didn't flinch—not once. He refused to be crushed by the weight of what was unfolding. While everything around him seemed to be crumbling, he remained anchored in belief, certain that even this season of suffering would pass. He prayed, he praised, and he kept going. His quiet strength became our shelter, a place where we could still breathe. Watching him bury child after child shattered something inside me. It broke me in ways I didn't know I could be broken. And still, I feared I might be next. That maybe my absence would one day be the subject of the next whisper.

But somehow, God carried us—through the haze, through the heartbreak. Not away from the fire, but through it.

No matter how much you hurt or grieve, the world doesn't wait. Life moves forward, demanding attention, decisions, action. And so, with too much to do and too little time, I had to carry on with the plans. Canaan was baptised—a moment of grace breaking through the heavy cloud of grief that still hung over us.

My friends showed up once again, just as they had for all three burials. Through every loss, they had been my constant—standing beside me in quiet strength, offering what they could, when they could. Their presence reminded me, as always, that I was not alone.

Meanwhile, the bridal shop, Belle Marie, was slowly beginning to pick up. Clients trickled in, offering me a glimmer of hope, but even as I felt a flicker of optimism, the doubt crept in. What if there were no brides for months? How would we survive?

Joan, especially, didn't want me to leave the shop. We had poured so much hard work into establishing it, and I could feel the weight of that effort in her voice every time she encouraged me to stay. But deep down, I knew running a business like this without a consistent income source would be a challenge, especially with three growing children and bills. God had given me a way out, a chance for a fresh start, and I knew I had to take it. If I didn't, I feared I would be left with nothing but "had I known" regrets.

Yet, the shop became more than just a business. It transformed into a sanctuary. Joan and other friends would stop by after work, filling the space with laughter and light-hearted conversations. I always looked forward to these moments. They allowed me to briefly forget the weight of my circumstances, offering me a few hours of peace in the warmth of their company.

At times, some would drop by to check in on me, offering support in ways I hadn't even expected—groceries, fuel for my car, or little blessings in whatever form they could give. Though I had my needs, God used my friends as His instruments, ensuring I never lacked the basics. There was always someone, or sometimes two, who would step in each day, reminding me that even in the hardest moments, I was not alone.

At home, Justine held down the fort, caring for the boys with her quiet unwavering dedication that had become her hallmark. She cared for the boys as if they were her own, ensuring that despite the turbulence of our circumstances, they still had a sense of stability. My trusted *boda boda* guy, Dan, took on the responsibility of picking them up from school each day. In Uganda, *boda bodas*—motorcycle taxis—are the pulse of daily life. They weave through the city's notorious traffic, offering a fast, affordable, and often unpredictable mode of transport. They are both a lifeline and a risk, a necessity in a place where time and road congestion rarely work in your favour. Everyone has their *boda* guy—someone they trust, someone they can count on. Mine was called Dan. A relationship that had gradually grown over the years. He was honest and ever dependable with any tasks and errands I asked him to run for me. Most importantly, Dan ensured Joshua and Caleb got home safely, a small but crucial link in the fragile balance we had managed to create.

Some days, the boys would come home and tell me they had seen Raymond drive past them as they rode with Dan. Their little voices, full of innocent confusion, would ask, "Why can't he come and live with us? Why doesn't he stop Dan and drive us?" Questions I had no answers to. So, I would deflect—ask about their day, crack a joke, or find them a treat, anything to steer their minds away from the questions that had no gentle answers. I was trying to protect them, trying not to break their hearts, even as mine quietly fractured a little more each time. The image haunted me. Their father, behind the windscreen, distant, separate—his life moving in a direction that no longer included us. It was a painful reminder of how much had changed, of how life could shift so drastically, leaving behind only ripples of what used to be.

Sometimes I wondered, how was it possible that he felt nothing? Did he actually feel... What had happened that was so terrible it had stripped him of the instinct to care for his own children? With us—him and me—I could almost understand. We were adults and maybe he had his reasons to do what he did. Maybe pain had hardened him, or resentment had taken root. But the children... they were innocent. They hadn't asked to be here. We—both of us—had made that decision. How could he not see them? Not reach for them? Not show up?

The more I thought, the more my heart ached under the weight of questions that had no satisfying answers. Had he ever truly been loved? Was he shown tenderness as a child, or did he learn early on that detachment was survival? Had life hardened him beyond reach?

But even that thought brought no peace—only sadness. I wanted to understand, but some truths stayed hidden, buried beneath years I hadn't lived and wounds I hadn't seen. I tried to forgive, but forgiveness did not erase the ache.

And yet, we carried on. Somehow, through unsaid worries and the looming goodbyes, life continued. Each day brought me one step closer to my departure—a journey into the unknown. I had no sureties for what lay ahead, only the conviction that I had to go. Even in my fear, I knew this was the only way forward.

In the days that followed, I sold my car and received a generous top-up from Joan's mother—my bonus mum, Mummy Jane. With this, I was able to pay a few months' rent and stock up on groceries to help Justine and the boys get by for a while. I also bought my ticket on June 25, 2014. With that secured, there was no turning back. Without me ever asking, Norah and her husband, Grace, graciously gave me access to a car when they knew I had sold mine, to help me as there was still a lot to do and less time. I was never left struggling; somewhere, somehow, God made a way—I did not lack.

"Your Father knoweth what things ye have need of, before ye ask him." —Matthew 6:8 (KJV)

The journey had begun, and I knew in my heart this was the best decision I could make with all that was surrounding me.

With all the preparations for my departure finalised, I had to summon every ounce of strength for one last, deeply important conversation with my parents. How do you tell the people who gave you life that you're leaving them behind? That you're going to a faraway country, and you don't know when—if ever—you'll return? knowing it will break their hearts? They were still alive, still holding on, even after everything life had thrown at them. And now, after all they had endured, I was about to bring them more pain.

Worse still, how was I to explain that I was leaving my children too? That I was going to another country without them, and their father—who should have been there—was not even in the picture?

How do you begin a conversation like that? The questions pressed heavily on my chest. Would they think I had given up? Would they understand that this wasn't a decision made out of ease or convenience, but out of necessity—one final attempt at building something better for all of us?

The thought tormented me. I was their daughter. I was a mother. And yet, I was choosing to walk away, even temporarily, from those I loved most. What kind of person did that make me? Would they ever understand? Could they?

This was not a farewell I could take lightly. I asked Patrick to come with me. I needed someone by my side—not to speak for me, but to steady me when words failed. The sorrow of leaving my ageing parents, uncertain if I'd ever hold them again, combined with the ache of separating from my children, was almost unbearable. And yet, it had to be done.

We planned. We travelled. And when the moment came, I told them.

Looking into my father's eyes as the weight of my words settled on him was one of the hardest things I've ever had to do. The sadness that welled up in them nearly undid me. I had always feared that each visit home might be our last, but this time—that fear clung to me with a heavy, unrelenting certainty. There was something final in the air, something I couldn't shake. And yet, even as the truth landed like a quiet storm between us, my parents didn't ask the questions I had braced myself for.

They didn't ask how long I'd be gone, or how I could leave my children behind. They didn't ask why I had chosen to go so far away.

I think, with age, comes a kind of wisdom that doesn't always need words. Maybe they had already seen the dead ends closing in around me—the strain of David's absence, the weight of a broken marriage, the demands of raising young children without a steady income or dependable help. They knew. Perhaps, deep within them, they even admired my courage—my desperate willingness to risk it all for the sake of my children's future.

Instead, they asked just one thing—the question that truly mattered to them: "Who are you leaving the children with?" Who would care for them? Who would look after them?

I knew that telling them I was leaving the children with Justine alone would send their hearts racing with worry. But before I could say a word, Patrick stepped in. He knew. With calm assurance, he answered, "She's leaving them with me." That response settled them—a bit, I think. It was enough for the moment.

Before we left, I found my way back to my father's room.

The house had fallen into that strange hush that often precedes a farewell—quiet but full, like the air itself was holding its breath.

After the routine midday prayers, he had stood up—slowly, carefully—leaning on the crutches that helped steady his steps in his later years. Each step was measured, his frame thinner now, his movements deliberate but dignified. Then, without saying much, he had made his way to his bedroom.

It was his nature, especially as he aged. Whenever he heard news that struck a nerve—news that might evoke tears he didn't want seen—he would quietly retreat to his bed. He never made a fuss, never demanded comfort. He simply removed himself from the moment and returned to the quiet sanctuary of his thoughts. There, he'd turn on the radio—often tuned to BBC or a local station—and lie back, facing up, staring into the air above him, lost in reflection.

I understood this about him. I had seen it many times before.

And I knew exactly where I'd find him.

My relationship with him had always been deeply special. We both knew it. We didn't have to say it often, though we did, in the ways that mattered. I knew how much he loved me, and he knew I adored him.

Every time I visited, we would spend endless evenings talking—long after others had gone to bed. We'd sit for hours discussing current affairs, sharing perspectives on everything from local politics to global shifts. BBC World News was his favourite. He was never formally educated—not a day of school in his life—but his literacy, his intellect, his understanding of the world was sharper than many I've met with degrees. He had taught himself to read and write, taught himself how the world moved, and taught me the value of staying informed.

We'd often talk from our separate beds, voices drifting through the house long into the night. Our rooms were across from each other, but it didn't matter. The conversations flowed easily—deep, curious, and often humorous—until one of us was eventually stolen by sleep. Those nights were special. And they belonged only to us.

He was going to miss me terribly—I could see it, feel it, almost hear it in the way he had gone quiet that afternoon. He would miss my cheeky teasing, my stories, my presence in the house. And I—I was going to miss him more than I could say. The most shattering part of it all was the unspoken question hanging in the air between us: Would we ever see each other again?

We both knew it was possible that we wouldn't. We didn't ask the question aloud. We didn't need to. We both knew.

So I walked to his room and stood at the doorway. He was lying on his back, eyes open, the radio murmuring softly beside him. I stepped in, crossed the space, and knelt beside his bed.

I wasn't just kneeling physically—I was kneeling in spirit. I had come for his blessing, just as Jacob's sons had knelt before him, receiving their father's final words before each stepped into their destinies.

"And Jacob called unto his sons, and said, Gather yourselves together, that I may tell you that which shall befall you in the last days."
— *Genesis 49:1 (KJV)*

He turned his head and looked at me, his eyes still holding that spark of humour that never left him.

"So… kneeling like one of Jacob's sons?" he said, that mischievous smile tugging at the corner of his mouth. "Should I start naming tribes?"

I laughed.

Then he added with a knowing grin, "You know people only kneel like this when the old man is on his way out."

It was a joke, yes—but also not. We laughed, that soft kind of laughter that knows sorrow is standing quietly in the same room, watching.

Then, still smiling, he laid his hands on me and began to pray.

He prayed with the depth of a father's love and the faith of a man who had known God through valleys and mountaintops. He asked the Lord to bless me in the land of Australia, to guide my steps, to grant me favour:

"Every place that the sole of your foot shall tread upon, that have I given unto you."
— *Joshua 1:3 (KJV)*

He prayed that those who blessed me would be blessed, and those who cursed me would be cursed:

"And I will bless them that bless thee, and curse him that curseth thee."
— *Genesis 12:3 (KJV)*

And then he prayed for all of his children—calling each of us by name, lifting us to God like an offering. He prayed for protection, provision, and peace.

I had asked Patrick to record that moment. I didn't fully understand why, but some part of me knew it was holy.

If ever I missed his voice too much, I thought, *I'll watch this. I'll listen. I'll remember.*

And in that room, kneeling beside him, wrapped in his words and prayers, I felt both the sorrow of leaving and the strength to go. Something in the atmosphere shifted. I wasn't walking away empty—I was being sent. Spiritually clothed in his blessing, I rose with tears in my eyes but a strange stillness in my spirit. I was ready.

My mother and I sobbed quietly, the kind of shared grief that says more in silence than words ever could. She didn't try to stop me. She didn't ask me to stay. But her eyes—those eyes that had watched me grow, stumble, rise again—were heavy with a sorrow only a mother could carry. I think she knew this moment had to happen, yet it didn't soften the pain of it. She had spent a lifetime strengthening me, and now she had to watch me go.

One of the two hardest goodbyes was behind me—or so I thought.

The truth is, I knew the last goodbye—to my children—would be far more shattering. I had rehearsed all the noble reasons in my mind: this sacrifice was for them. I was offering myself to carry the cross of separation, to carve out a path in the wilderness. But none of that made the ache of parting feel any lighter. The image of their small faces lingered in my thoughts like a whisper I could never quiet.

I had told myself that this was my offering. That God sees. That somehow, it would count.

Patrick and I left together. By now, he was more than just a brother—he was a companion in this exile of sorts, a silent strength walking beside me. He carried some of the emotional weight I couldn't name, just by being there. That day, he became a bridge between what I was leaving and what I hoped to find.

"A friend loveth at all times, and a brother is born for adversity."
— *Proverbs* 17:17 (KJV)

What are brothers for, if not for moments like this? I didn't take it as metaphor—I took it literally. Patrick was born for this moment.

To steady me. To speak when I could not. To walk beside me as I left everything that mattered.

He knew I didn't have the words, and so he offered his presence instead. His answers where mine failed. His steadiness where mine wavered. I don't think he'll ever know how deeply I leaned on that.

The truth is, I have never been one to burden others with my struggles. Even when my tribe of faithful friends rallied around me—always showing up, always doing more than I could ever ask—I rarely let them carry my fears. They gave out of love, not obligation. And I believe that God's favour is a garment; when you are clothed in it, as I believe my life is, things happen you don't necessarily deserve. It's an unfair advantage—stamped by heaven.

And as unconventional as it may have seemed to others, I found peace in knowing my children were with Justine. It takes a different kind of faith to entrust your most precious ones to someone whose history you haven't combed through, whose life you've never fully investigated. I had never run a background check. I didn't ask for references. But I knew. There was a peace in my spirit. I rested in trust, because that's what faith demands—obedience without full clarity.

Faith doesn't follow logic. Sometimes, it just leaps.

From the moment she entered our lives and shared her story—a story marked by unimaginable injustice and trauma—I knew God had sent her to test my faith. Her past was a shadow that seemed to follow her relentlessly, an unwanted burden no one should carry. To believe in her, to entrust my children to her care, demanded a faith beyond reason, a faith fierce enough to hold onto hope when all logic said otherwise.

I made a promise to God: to treat her with the kindness and fairness He requires of me. In return, I prayed that He would use her as an instrument of His will to protect and nurture my children. When the time came to make the life-altering decision, I reminded

God of that prayer. In that moment, I surrendered my children to Him—not just in words, but from the deepest place in my heart. They had never truly been mine to keep; I was only their steward. And it is that surrender that gave me the courage to take the steps I did.

The day of departure arrived.

I packed my entire life into a single suitcase weighing no more than twenty-three kilograms. With that small bag, I left behind everything I had ever known—my children, my friends, my home, and the familiar comforts that had shaped my world. It hurt to leave them all, especially my youngest, Canaan, who was just eighteen months old. His tiny frame and trusting eyes made the goodbye almost unbearable. Joshua and Caleb were never far from my thoughts; their faces and laughter were held close to my heart.

Leaving them was painful beyond words. The ache of parting from my baby—so fragile, so utterly dependent—stayed with me. His soft breaths, the warmth of his little hands, the way he clung to me with innocent trust—all of it lingered in my mind. Yet despite the deep pain, I moved forward with fierce resolve, holding tightly to faith and hope that this sacrifice would create a path for our reunion. The future was unseen, but I believed in it with all my heart.

With political unrest tightening its grip like a slow-burning fuse, I couldn't risk being detained at the airport. I didn't know who in my family might be a target and who might be spared. So, I slipped away on a night bus bound for Kenya, hidden beneath the cover of darkness, walking straight into a future that was far from clear.

The final goodbye unfolded under the muted lights of the night. Dr Doreen took me to the bus with the boys, Justine, and Ozzy. That moment—standing there, knowing it was the final goodbye—was one I savoured for as long as I could before letting go. I held each hug tighter, every word spoken stretching across time and space, unsure if or when I'd ever see them again. Life guarantees nothing, and I was deeply aware of that. I let go only because I had to—not because I was ready.

Ozzy, my dear friend, refused to let me go alone. He travelled with me all the way to Nairobi, determined to see me through safely. We both knew too well how quickly things could spiral. The bus ride was long and silent, each of us wrapped in our own thoughts. Every checkpoint felt like a gamble. Every glance from an officer made my heart race. But by morning, we had arrived.

Beatrice was waiting. She welcomed me into her home with a warmth I didn't realise I needed so much. That evening, she made dinner, and we sat together, sifting through the weight of it all—what was at hand, what I hoped for, the barriers ahead, the unspoken fears, the great expectations. A tangled mix of everything.

When morning came, it was time. There was no turning back. Beatrice drove me to the airport. She kept encouraging me, reminding me of my courage and the strength it had taken to come this far. She was visibly moved, knowing what it meant for a mother to do what I had done. She and Ozzy bid me farewell as I boarded the Emirates flight to Melbourne, my heart caught between the pain of parting and the quiet dream of a new beginning.

Ozzy returned home to reassure Justine, my children, and our friends that I had made it safely onto the plane—that there had been no trouble or incident. That, for now, the hardest part was behind us. And though hope and faith were all I had to hold onto, even those—on some days—felt impossibly delicate.

I had no idea how long it would take to settle in the new continent—how long anything would take. No one does. Each journey is unique. There's no formula, no single story that fits us all. Most of all, I didn't know when I would be with my children again. I only knew that every step I took was for them.

PART IV:

A NEW LAND, A NEW LIFE

AUSTRALIA HERE I COME!

I landed in Melbourne on the morning of July 20th, 2014, at exactly 7:50 a.m.—right in the heart of winter. You might wonder how I remember the time so precisely after all these years. I still have the boarding pass and ticket tucked safely away. They're worn and creased now, but to me, they're sacred—my stones of remembrance. Like the children of Israel, who were instructed never to forget the day the Lord brought them out, I, too, held onto these as a testimony. They are proof that I crossed over.

But the truth is, it didn't feel like a fresh start. Not yet. I had crossed oceans and borders, left behind my children, my home, my past—but I carried it all with me. My grief, my longing, my unanswered questions—they clung to me like the winter cold that met me at the gate.

Melbourne's winter isn't loud. It doesn't arrive in blizzards or thunder. It creeps in quietly, chilling your bones with sharp winds and grey skies that sit low over the city like a heavy sigh. That morning, the air bit through the layers I had wrapped myself in. My fingers stiffened as I clutched my documents, and each breath felt like it froze somewhere deep inside my chest. Even the light was cold, silvery and subdued, casting long shadows across the airport floor. I had stepped into a new world—but everything in me was still bracing for what might go wrong.

The flight itself had been long and thick with nerves. From the moment I boarded, I felt hyper-aware of everything—every glance from a flight attendant, every sideways look from a fellow passenger. I kept expecting something to go wrong. To be pulled aside. To be questioned. To be turned back. It felt like this was going too well, and something was bound to interrupt it. I couldn't believe it was happening—that I was en route to another life, another land, another chance.

It reminded me of Abraham, when God told him to leave everything behind—his land, his people, his father's house—and go to a place that God would show him. A place not yet revealed. That story had always stirred something in me, but now I understood it differently. Surely even Abraham, great as his faith was, must have had a "huh" moment. Not doubt, but a deep breath kind of anticipation. A nervous trust. That's how it felt for me. Physically anxious. Spiritually hopeful.

Walking into customs, my stomach tightened into a knot that wouldn't release. Every official, every sign, every line I stood in—it all felt unreal. I was holding my breath, expecting at any moment to be stopped, questioned, turned around. But step by step, no one did.

I had arrived.

And though I didn't know what came next—how long it would take for life to make sense again, or when I would hold my children—I knew that this moment, this crossing, would never be forgotten. Not because it was triumphant, but because it was faithful.

And faith, after all, had brought me this far.

My heart pounded with fear, and my breath got caught in my chest as if I were standing on the edge of something too vast to comprehend. I was nervous, scared and dazed by the emotional turmoil of everything I had lived through.

The pain of the past few years—no, the weight of that single year alone felt like a heavy cloak, suffocating me, freezing my very soul. Every step I took seemed to be dictated by the ghosts of all that I had lost, the scars of the heartache I had carried. My emotional state was raw, fragile, and too worn to embrace anything but the brutal reality of my struggles.

And yet, here I was—standing in a new place, a place that should have been filled with tangible hope and promise. Instead, it felt like I was expected to pick up a toolbox, to begin peeling back layer after layer of hardship just to survive. It wasn't a fresh start. It was another battle in a war I had been fighting for far too long. Every moment felt like I was trying to make sense of a life that had broken apart, unsure of what could possibly come next, but knowing I had no choice but to forge ahead.

I thank God for that morning. The airport was a hive of movement— people rushing past, luggage wheels humming across the floor, long lines snaking through customs and security. People were everywhere, yet somehow, in the middle of it all, I felt strangely still—shielded, almost. I was nervous but strangely calm, like I had been wrapped in something invisible but strong.

I was cleared through customs so swiftly, I barely had time to absorb it. When I reached for my suitcase, ready to unzip it for inspection, the officer barely looked at me. "No need," he said, waving me through without a second glance.

What a relief.

That moment—so small to anyone else—was everything to me. It was grace. Mercy. My garment of favour.

You might not see it that way, but standing there, I did. I knew exactly what could have happened. One wrong answer, one misplaced word, one nervous glance—it would've been enough to raise suspicion. I could've been pulled aside. Questioned. Sent back. And honestly, if that officer had asked me anything at all, I probably would've frozen like a deer in headlights. Not out of guilt, but sheer fear. My nerves were so raw, it wouldn't have taken much.

But he didn't ask.

He just waved me through.

God's favour. It covered me that morning, plain and simple. And while others may have seen just another traveller passing through, I knew better. I knew I had just walked through a gate that only God could have opened.

Pause for a minute—have you been to Australia? Just before you touch down, they drill the biosecurity laws into you like a final warning before judgment day. Declare everything. No exceptions. The penalties for getting it wrong? Steep fines, confiscations, and if you mess up—prosecution. It's enough to make even the most innocent traveller second-guess every item in their bag. You start to eye your suitcase like it's hiding secrets.

Then came the dreaded declaration form. If it's your first time, you stare at it like a trick question on an exam where failure could get you deported.

Food? No.

Medicine? Well… does ibuprofen count—or is that now a controlled substance?

Wooden items? My souvenir keychain is carved from wood… does sentimentality make it exempt?

And the questions only get worse:

Have you been on a farm in the last 30 days?

Well, not officially. But the journey out of Uganda involved passing goats, chickens, cows, and several open fields that definitely weren't shopping malls.

Have you been in contact with freshwater streams, lakes, or wild animals?

Technically yes—if washing your feet in a river counts as contact. If so, then I'm guilty as charged.

Have you been to Africa, South America, or the Caribbean in the last six days?

I'm from Africa. What would you like me to tick?

Are you carrying any animal products, soil, or plant material?

Let's see... I've got tea leaves, a wooden bracelet, and the lingering scent of red earth and eucalyptus in my clothes.

So I did what the form advised: *If unsure, declare it.*

It seemed safer to admit to everything—and let them sort out what mattered—than to say no and end up explaining myself over a teabag. I wasn't about to play roulette with Australian customs.

I imagined myself in a cold, sterile room, trying to explain why my dusty shoes or a forgotten protein bar buried at the bottom of my bag weren't a threat to national biosecurity. That image alone was enough to convince me—I didn't want to end up there. That's why I declared. Everything I could think of. Because the real weight wasn't just in the form—it was in what I carried deep within. The unspoken truth that I wasn't just here for a short course, a conference, or a friendly visit. I was here to stay. To begin again, from scratch.

If that customs officer had access to my thoughts—if they could read the quiet, unwavering resolve in my heart—would they have let me in? Would they have seen the desperation, the fragile hope, the fierce determination? I doubt it. I'm certain my visa would've been cancelled on the spot. I'd have been rerouted to a detention centre—or placed on the next plane out.

Thank God we don't walk around with our intentions printed across our foreheads.

So when the officer barely glanced at my bag and waved me through without a single question, the relief hit me like a flood. That was it. I was in. For better or worse, it was now me—and my will to make this work. There was no going back.

The arrival waiting area was a blur of movement. Families, couples and friends embracing, weary travellers dragging suitcases, voices overlapping in a dozen languages. My eyes scanned the crowd until they landed on Joseph. Relief flooded through me. A familiar face in a foreign land. I let out a breath I hadn't even realised I was holding. I wasn't alone.

As I walked toward him, he looked at me in surprise. "You got through quickly," he said, glancing around at the packed terminal. The sheer number of people that morning made my swift passage through customs feel almost unreal. But there I was, standing before him—past the checkpoints, past the scrutiny, past the unspoken fears. I had made it.

We walked to the car where his wife, Nicole, was waiting, her hands resting gently on her belly—she was expecting their first child, Luca. The sight of them, a growing family was a reminder of life moving forward, of new beginnings unfolding in different ways.

The cold air outside the airport bit into my skin sharp and unfamiliar. It felt like standing on the edge of a cliff, staring into a world I had imagined a thousand times but was only now stepping into. This was starting to look and feel like a new life in every sense. No more "if only this or that." No more wondering. I was here. And I had to make good on the promises I had made to myself.

As we drove to their home in regional Victoria, my mind replayed the countless conversations Joseph and I had had over the years about life in Australia. What to expect, how to navigate the system, the do's and don'ts. Now, those conversations weren't just theory. This was real. And I needed a plan. A proper plan.

I spent the first week at Joseph and Nicole's home regrouping, catching my breath, and preparing for what lay ahead. More than anything, I needed to start the 866 visa application process as quickly as possible. If there was one thing I learned right away, it was that applying for protection in Australia wasn't just about filling out forms—it was about building a case, layer by layer, proving in painstaking detail why going back home was not an option.

The application demands more than just a statement; it requires a full account of your life. Who you are, where you come from, what you have endured, and—most importantly—why you cannot go back. Every claim must be backed by evidence. Dates, names, incidents, supporting documents, news articles—anything that can substantiate your story. The weight of it is crushing. You are asked to relive, in writing, the very things you are running from.

It felt like reopening wounds that had barely begun to close. And yet, that was the requirement. To lay it all bare. Then, after pouring out every painful detail, I would have to wait for years—for a decision that could either grant me a future or send me back to the very place I had fled. The thought of writing it all down made my chest tighten. But there was no turning back. This was the moment to fight for the life I had dared to believe was possible.

Thank God for these good people. They didn't just feed and shelter me, they gave me space to think, to process, to put my thoughts into words and write them down. Joseph, knowing the process inside and out, guided me through it all. He showed me what details mattered most in my application, the forms I needed to fill out, and the kind of evidence that could make or break my case. If there was one person who stood by me as I stepped into this new life, it was him.

I remember confiding in him about both the possibilities and the fears—the uphill struggle to raise the money for my ticket, and the terrifying thought that I might never make it out. What if I was arrested on my way out of the country? What if I disappeared into a government safe house, tortured into silence, and my children were left with no answers, no hope of ever seeing me again? These weren't wild imaginations—they were very real, very possible outcomes.

He listened quietly, then said, "You must do what you have to do—or at least try. Sitting around thinking of everything that could go wrong won't change anything. You need to try, while there's still time."

Then came the matter of my car. I hoped he'd offer to help. But his words were firm: "I won't give you the money—even though I could. And it's not because I'm being mean. It's because you need to understand what you're sacrificing. You need to value this journey. You can't afford to look back."

At the time, his words stung. I didn't see the wisdom in them. But sitting in that room, preparing to write the hardest story of my life, I understood. He was right. I was here, and there was no looking back. There were no comforts to cling to, no easy way out. Even my most precious treasures—my children—were out of reach. If I had to fight for a future, then I had to be all in.

Forms downloaded, I began the painstaking process of filling them out and writing my statement. I wrote and wrote, pouring my story onto those pages as if my very future depended on it—because it did.

Looking back, I sometimes wonder if I should have held back—or at least been more measured in what I disclosed. Not that they wouldn't have found the information elsewhere, but in my eagerness to lay it all out, I opened a door—a door that invited scrutiny, questions from every angle, even about things I hadn't considered. My siblings' death certificates? Imagine having to contact their grieving families for copies. Daniel's post-mortem report? Really? Proof of this, evidence of that—it all became part of the process.

But at the time, I felt I had no choice. Holding back wasn't an option. David was still making headlines in international media, and I knew that if I left any gaps—no matter how personal or sensitive—they would be filled by someone else, likely in ways that stripped away my dignity and distorted my truth. An article, a soundbite, a misquoted phrase pulled out of context could be enough to jeopardise everything. So, I told them everything. Every painful truth. Every risk. Every reason why going back was not just difficult—but impossible. I thought transparency would strengthen my case, show good faith, speed up the process and help me reunite with my children sooner.

I was willing to lay myself bare.

Had I known what I was inviting, I might have been more careful with what I wrote—said less. Not to withhold the truth, but to wait until I was asked. Sometimes, offering too much too soon doesn't strengthen your case—it complicates it.

"*A fool uttereth all his mind: but a wise man keepeth it in till afterwards.*" (Proverbs 29:11, KJV)

Not every truth needs to be written all at once. Sometimes, wisdom lies in letting the questions come first.

A CITY, A CENTRE, A SECOND CHANCE

The days flew by in a blur, and before I knew it, the real test was upon me. Joseph, ever the pillar of support, took the day off on Friday to take me to Melbourne. We travelled together, and with every stop, the sense of what was coming settled deeper in my chest.

Soon, we arrived at Footscray Station—my stop. We got off, and he walked me to the entrance of the Asylum Seeker Resource Centre. There was a bench right outside. I sat there briefly as he explained that this was it. I had to walk in, ask for help, and start again. He handed me a small slip of paper—with train lines, platforms, and the contact details of services that might be of assistance. Then, standing beside me at the entrance, he looked me in the eye and said, "This is it."

He had already done so much—painted me the dream of Australia, told me what a wonderful place it was, and spoke hope into my heart that I wouldn't just survive here, but thrive. He had offered me shelter, guidance, and support when I had none. But the next step was mine alone.

I watched him walk away. Swallowed hard. Turned to face the building in front of me.

The weekend was looming. I knew no one in Melbourne. I had no accommodation, no food, no certainty about what came next. But there was no time for fear.

I stepped through the doors, walked up to the reception desk and, with as much steadiness as I could muster, introduced myself. My voice felt small, yet firm. And just like that, the next chapter of my journey began.

The waiting area was full—faces from different corners of the world, each carrying their own stories of escape, survival, and desperate hope. Some sat quietly, others whispered among themselves, but the weight of uncertainty hung thick in the air. We were all here for the same reason: seeking help, seeking a chance.

When my turn came, I registered my details. A kind volunteer soon came to assist me. The Asylum Seeker Resource Centre (ASRC) was more than a service—it was a lifeline. A refuge. Here, asylum seekers weren't reduced to case numbers or applications. We were seen. Heard. Given dignity, without judgment. From legal aid to food, emergency accommodation, and emotional support, the ASRC stood in the gap for people who had nowhere else to turn.

That Friday, ASRC immediately sprang into action. They contacted HomeGround, a housing service, but there was no capacity that evening. I braced myself for bad news, but ASRC didn't let us walk away empty-handed. They arranged temporary accommodation for the weekend at a backpackers' hostel—for me and others in similar situations. They gave us public transport passes, basic groceries, and a bag of essentials.

It wasn't much, but it was everything.

I clutched my suitcase and the shopping bag they'd given me. My mind was already racing ahead to Monday. There was still so much to figure out. I needed to lodge my application, find a lawyer, and formalise my legal standing. But most pressingly, I needed long-term accommodation. I had no income, no job, no family in Melbourne. Apart from Joseph and Nicole—who had already done more than enough—I knew no one here. I would need help from anywhere and anyone willing to give it.

For now, though, I had somewhere to sleep and something to eat. That, in itself, was a blessing.

The backpackers' hostel was chaotic—a constant stream of strangers drifting in and out. Some were travellers; others, like me, were simply displaced. The space was mixed-gender, with little privacy. But it was a bed, a roof, a pause in the madness. That night, I curled into myself, exhaustion pulling me under—but gratitude held me steady. It was Friday night. And someone had made sure I wasn't sleeping on the street.

Later that evening, Joseph called to check on how I had gone. He was relieved to hear I had found a place to stay and had been able to get some assistance. I sat with that relief, knowing he and Nicole had already done so much for me. I hadn't even mentioned that when I first arrived, they bought me a SIM card and helped set it up—so I could reach my children back home. That one act alone meant everything. Even from across the world, even with the unknown hanging over me, I could still hear my children's voices.

That, more than anything, kept me going.

Over the following days, I began to meet others at the ASRC. We bonded over meals, shared stories, and exchanged fragments of our lives—people navigating journeys both strikingly similar and vastly different from mine. Some had fled war, persecution, domestic violence, or economic collapse. Some had left children behind, like I had. Others had arrived alone, carrying nothing but exhaustion and hope.

Making friends had always come naturally to me, so I leaned into that. That's how I met Mahlet. Her laughter, warm face, and easy presence drew me in immediately. I still remember our very first conversation—I asked her, straight out, "Can we be friends?"

Just like that. And somehow, that was all it took. We were in this together from that moment on. She became my confidant, a steady companion through it all, and a friend for life. Every chance we had to catch up, we found something to laugh about, to lighten the heaviness of what we were carrying.

Then I met Sylvia. We were introduced through a mutual connection—Peace—who had been introduced to me by Joseph. One morning, Sylvia and I found ourselves taking the same train to the ASRC, as had quickly become the rhythm of the week. As we walked from the station, our conversation drifted to our children. I said to her, "At least you have Danny," referring to her youngest son. The moment the words left my mouth, I broke down in tears.

My boys were far away, in limbo, caught in a waiting game with no clear end. I didn't know when—or if—I'd see them again.

Without a word, Sylvia reached into her bag and handed me a small note. "Send it to them," she said.

It wasn't much. But in that moment, it was everything. A simple gesture that carried the weight of love, solidarity, and understanding.

FOOTSCRAY
A Mini-Africa in Melbourne

Life moved forward, and the next season unfolded with relentless motion. Footscray—vibrant, layered, and alive—became my daily hub of activity. Predominantly home to African and Vietnamese communities, it felt like a cultural intersection: a bridge between the world I had come from and the uncertain ground I was learning to stand on.

Though I didn't live there, Footscray offered something deeper than familiarity—it offered connection. It was a mosaic of language, scent, sound, and memory. In many ways, it felt like a recreated Vietnamese and African village, thriving in the heart of another continent.

My regular visits to the area were more than just errands or appointments at the ASRC—because that's where it was located. This suburb, with its vibrant community, gave me hope. The scent of African spices mingled with the hum of hair salons and the chatter spilling from shopfronts. I didn't need to know each person's story, but every face I passed in a shop, café, or restaurant carried a quiet vibe of resilience. If so many of them had made it in this country, I could too.

My accommodation, like so much else at that time, was transitory. I was placed with others in similar circumstances at a backpackers' hostel called Urban Central in Southbank, the cost covered week by week. Yet even this modest provision came with a caveat: every Friday, we were required to report to either HomeGround or the ASRC. The purpose was clear, though quietly dehumanising—we had to prove we were still at risk of homelessness, to justify continued support.

That ritual, though necessary, underscored the precariousness of it all. Still, between those two services, I found enough to keep going. At ASRC, I was supported by a team of caseworkers—individuals who, in every sense, became a steady source of help. From food and clothing to Myki cards and travel top-ups, their care extended far beyond practical aid. Their presence was stabilising, their belief in dignity unshaken.

What moved me most was the spirit in which they served. Many of them were retired professionals who chose to spend their days helping others, or young social work students on placement, eager to learn and make a difference. Their compassion wasn't performative—it was rooted, quiet, and profound. In my most uncertain moments, their kindness stood like a lighthouse. I remain deeply grateful to ASRC—not just for what they gave, but for how they gave it. Their holistic approach transformed survival into something almost sacred: a shared human experience where hope was not just offered, but made tangible.

One of the first significant steps in my asylum journey was securing a bridging visa. Gerald, a friend of Joseph's, was a student at Victoria University's Footscray campus—a stone's throw from ASRC. He played a pivotal role in finalising my 866 visa application, guiding me through the process of submitting it and handling the payment at the post office. Shortly afterwards, I think in the week that followed, I received an acknowledgment letter confirming a valid visa application. With it came my Bridging Visa A (BVA), granting me work and study rights. It was a moment worth celebrating—a step towards autonomy. Not all bridging visas offer such freedoms. Some asylum seekers find themselves on Bridging Visa E (BVE), which often comes with restrictions, including the inability to work or study. This leaves individuals in prolonged limbo, unable to build a future while waiting for an outcome that could take years. Bridging visas, meant to provide temporary status while awaiting an immigration decision, vary greatly in their conditions. Some offer full rights to work and study, while others severely limit access to employment and education, pushing many into hardship. The uncertainty attached to them is a heavy burden, but for those who receive work rights, it becomes a chance to regain dignity and independence. Yet even with it, many privileges remained out of reach. I clung to every opportunity I could find, managing to secure access to essential services like Medicare. The need to renew it every three months became a constant reminder of how precarious my footing was—and of the relentless pursuit of stability in this new life.

With my visa application acknowledged, the next challenge was securing a pro bono lawyer to guide me through the legal intricacies of my case. To my surprise, this process was relatively straightforward. On my third call, Refugee Legal agreed to take on my case. They assigned me Lucy, a dedicated and knowledgeable lawyer who became my advocate. Unlike many others seeking asylum, my application was already in motion, leaving Lucy with little to do initially. The waiting game had begun—an unpredictable, often excruciating period before the next step: the immigration interview. The reality of this waiting period is sobering. Months, sometimes years, pass before any significant progress is made. I knew I had to find a way to be productive in the meantime.

Starting over in a foreign land without familiar foundations was daunting. With no job or income, every day felt like a leap of faith. Despite my education and qualifications, I didn't know where to begin—those would require an entirely different process. But I needed to get started as soon as possible to keep fulfilling my parental responsibilities back home. So, I had to begin working—trusting that every step, no matter how small, was still progress.

As I waited for the next steps in my immigration process, I started to think of avenues to study and gain employable skills. Work would provide not just financial relief but also a sense of purpose. Though nothing was guaranteed—neither permanent accommodation nor immediate stability—I refused to be helpless. Every small victory, from securing a Myki card to finding a meal, became a testament to the resilience and the power of support networks. The journey of seeking asylum is layered with complexities, from bureaucratic hurdles to emotional turmoil. But within this labyrinth of uncertainty, there are moments of grace—acts of kindness that remind us that humanity prevails even in the most challenging circumstances. My story is just one among many, a testament to the strength of those who continue to fight for a place to call home. And so, I moved forward, step by step, guided by the unwavering belief that a better future awaited.

DOOR KNOCKING FOR CHANGE

One morning, while having breakfast at Urban Central, I glanced at the hostel's notice board and saw various job postings. Many short-term accommodations displayed such ads, as employers knew that temporary residents, travellers, and asylum seekers were often in need of work. One particular listing caught my attention—a role with Plan International, a nonprofit organisation I was familiar with. Having known people in Uganda who had benefited from their sponsorship programs, I felt a connection to their cause. The job promised a chance to drive social change while earning a weekly wage of about $450 or thereabouts. Something is better than nothing, right? It seemed promising, so I took down the details and made contact.

The role required an immediate start, but first, I needed a bank account and a tax file number. And so, I did.

I had no clear idea what the actual work entailed, only that I would be part of a great team doing meaningful things. That was enough to excite me. It was only on the first day that I realised what the job involved—door-to-door fundraising. The challenge was twofold: first, memorising the entire mission of Plan International, and second, persuading strangers to commit to a monthly sponsorship of a child. It was sold to us as fun and easy, but in reality, it was gruelling work. We were trained to remind people that for just a dollar a day, they could change a child's life, transform communities, and make a global impact. But enthusiasm can only get you so far. Door-to-door fundraising is a tough gig—people generally don't appreciate uninvited visitors, and I quickly understood why even Jehovah's Witnesses face resistance when knocking on doors.

Each morning, Monday to Friday we gathered at the office near the Shrine of Remembrance, where we were hyped up with chants and slogans before being assigned our target areas for the day. A van would drop us off, and each of us was given a map outlining our designated turf. Our job was to knock on every door that didn't have a "Do Not Knock" sign and engage in persuasive conversations to secure sponsorships. It was exhausting, emotionally draining, and often demoralising. Some people were kind and listened, but many were indifferent or outright hostile. The cold Melbourne weather didn't help either.

After my first week, I was elated to receive my first paycheck—a tangible sign that I was making progress. Filled with hope, I shared the news and the opportunity with Tracy, an asylum seeker friend who lived with me at the backpackers, knowing how much it could mean for both of us. She joined the team, but the pressure of meeting daily sign-up quotas quickly became overwhelming. Failure to meet targets meant being let go. We lasted two weeks before deciding we couldn't keep up. The stress that came with the opportunity and constant rejection took its toll on our mental health. I knew that I had to find something better, safer and with a promise of more stability.

PASTOR CLAUDE

As if divinely orchestrated, help came just when I needed it most. God, in His mysterious ways, brought someone into my life who would change everything—the late Pastor Claude. They say God takes the good ones early, and Claude is no exception.

I met him through Peace, who had invited me to a small fellowship he had started in Ardeer. Peace and I had known each other for some time now. Like me, she was navigating her immigration struggles. Though she couldn't offer much practical support, she was a wellspring of information, always connecting me with helpful contacts.

Pastor Claude took a deep interest in my story, particularly the hardship of being separated from my children. His heart resolved to help, and his generosity soon extended to Tracy, Sylvia, and others. Recognising that securing stable work in Australia required certifications, he enrolled the three of us in a disability and aged care course. I often joke that in Australia, even climbing a tree requires a certificate—and it's not far from the truth.

Under his mentorship, I embarked on this pivotal course—a crucial step toward reintegration into the workforce. Beyond financing our studies, he ensured we had everything we needed and provided emotional support in moments of homesickness and loneliness. His kindness knew no bounds; he facilitated communication with our loved ones and imparted invaluable life skills like learning the road rules, understanding parking signs and overall driving in Australia. As an immigrant himself, he empathised deeply with our struggles and championed our cause tirelessly.

Tragically, his untimely demise robbed him of witnessing the fruits of his labour, leaving behind a void that words cannot fill. Yet, his legacy lives on in the countless lives he touched, including mine with enduring love, selflessness, and wisdom.

The aged care course, though short at six months, was transformative. One of its greatest blessings was the friendships I forged. Among them was meeting and connecting with Jane, the manual handling trainer and later her husband, Michael, the first aid trainer. Jane was warm, welcoming, and from East Africa—Kenya, to be specific. The Wanyama's became part of my growing support network. Over the years, this friendship has grown and they're more like family.

I remember one rainy day during placement, the downpour seemed relentless. Jane came to my rescue. She had come to supervise me at the aged care home where I was doing my placement. Jane offered me a ride back to my accommodation. Memories like these may seem like a simple occurrence but I see how God orchestrated every step of my journey. From small victories like securing work rights to life-changing encounters with people who shared their resources, love, and empathy—each moment was a thread woven into my story. In the depths of uncertainty, grace kept pursuing me. And so, I pressed on, knowing that a greater purpose was unfolding, even if I couldn't see it.

THE NEWS I DREADED

Life seemed to be moving in the right direction—and then the most devastating cataclysm hit me. It was a crisp Sunday evening in Melbourne, the kind that carried the scent of salt and eucalyptus on the breeze, with a dusky golden light spilling across the city. It was just after 7 p.m. here, which meant it was still early morning in Uganda. October 5th, 2014, would forever mark a turning point in my journey.

    I remember the moment with piercing clarity. I was perched on a bunk bed in a city backpackers' hostel, sharing the room with two lively German travellers whose laughter danced through the space, carrying the lightness of their day's adventures—to the Twelve Apostles on the Great Ocean Road. Then, my phone rang. It was my mother—a call that would change everything.

    I hesitated, as though letting it ring just a little longer could somehow delay the inevitable. I had a premonition—subtle, but unshakable. In our recent conversations, he had grown noticeably weaker. His voice, once vibrant and warm, had become faint, thinned by pain but thick with yearning. Each time we spoke, he would whisper, "*Just let me go… I want to go home.*"

    We had been praying for healing, pleading with heaven to restore him—but he was already gazing elsewhere. *Home*, for him, no longer meant the familiar places we clung to. It meant heaven. He was weary—of the struggle, the aches, the weight of life—but there was no fear in him, only a deep longing. In his frailty, there was still a certain light. He was ready.

So when the call came, I sensed its gravity. Something in my spirit recoiled with quiet, solemn dread. When I finally answered, her voice was calm—almost preternaturally so—like someone holding herself together with strands of faith and sheer will.

"Don't break," she began gently, "he has gone home... he is in glory now—free from pain, free from the burdens of this life."

She told me how it happened. That morning, like every other, they had gathered for devotion at 5 a.m. He led them in praise and worship—his voice still carrying a soft authority, lifted above the groans of his body. And then, with a glimmer of humour and a strange light in his eyes, he told them he was leaving. He smiled, said his goodbyes—"*See you in heaven*," he quipped, as though merely catching the next bus. Then he drifted off to sleep again.

And that was it.

He went quietly. Peacefully. Surrounded by her love, and by the presence of some of my siblings, nieces, and nephews—his legacy gathered near him as he slipped away.

But her words did not comfort me as much as she likely hoped. Instead, my world collapsed inward like a shattered prism. I rose quickly, slipping out the door and seating myself against the cold, unforgiving wall outside the room. I dared not break down in that confined space where others could see.

I was frozen—rigid and immobile. Void of emotion. I wanted to scream, to sob uncontrollably, to unravel under the crushing weight of it all—but my body betrayed me. I simply sat there, hollowed out and suspended in a cavernous silence, as the reality encroached relentlessly from every angle, dense and suffocating.

My limbs refused to obey; my mind recoiled in denial. I had dreaded this moment my entire life, playing it out in endless rehearsal, yet when it arrived, I was numb—ensnared in a stupor of disbelief.

Growing up, I had spun this scenario over and over in my mind, questioning how and where it would unfold. Would he pass quietly at home, or in the sterile coldness of a hospital? Would I be granted one last conversation, or would his departure be swift and unannounced? How would I say goodbye to my hero? These questions loomed like spectres, but nothing could have braced me for the crushing reality of being thousands of miles away when it happened. The weight of that distance was unbearable.

The words of Job reverberated deeply within my spirit:

"*What I feared hath come upon me; and that which I was afraid of is come unto me.*" (Job 3:25, KJV)

Here was a unique grief, born from absence—the cruel agony of not standing beside him in those final moments, of never seeing his face one last time, of not being wrapped in the shared sorrow of family. I felt untethered in my mourning, an exile in a foreign land, wrestling to comprehend an event so profound while the world around me carried on as if untouched.

That night is indelibly impressed upon my soul—each moment seared into the fabric of my memory. I remember calling Joseph, my voice barely a whisper, words laden with unbearable weight. The days that followed slipped by in a nebulous haze of grief—the world spinning onward while I remained suspended in sorrow's stillness.

Yet one thing stands out through the fog: my speech. I was grateful to have been able, in some small way, to send him off with the dignity and love he deserved. I wrote my heart into that speech and sent it to my niece Stella via WhatsApp, asking her to read it on my behalf. Every line was a labour of love—my way of honouring the man who had held my world, my moon, and my stars.

In that speech, I spoke of his unshakeable love for God—a love that was not confined to private devotion but poured into every corner of his life. He was never ashamed of the gospel and never too busy to serve. His faith was deep, loud, and alive. He carried it into his work, into his friendships, into his parenting, and into the heart of the community. Whether it was Sunday morning prayer or a conversation on a dusty roadside, he lived to witness Christ.

I spoke of his compassion for people, his kindness that knew no bounds. He gave without ever keeping count—time, money, food, shelter, wisdom. So many found refuge in his generosity, not just in physical ways, but in the way he made people feel seen, heard, and valued. He loved his neighbours as himself, and his door was always open.

I honoured his leadership—a rare and unassuming gravitas that did not rely on titles to command respect. He led with quiet conviction and a deep, intrinsic sense of duty. Whether within the family, the church, or the wider community, people followed him because they trusted him. His word was his covenant. A man whose yes was unshakably yes, and whose no was unalterably no. There was no artifice in him—only integrity worn like a second skin.

I spoke of his evangelism, not just in words but in how he lived. His life was his loudest sermon. He sowed seeds of faith in children, friends, strangers—anyone whose path crossed his. His love for scripture and singing hymns is still a sound imprinted in my spirit.

And I spoke of the ache—the deep, soul-tearing ache of not being home to bury him. Of watching it all unfold from a distance, helplessly. Of grieving across oceans. But I also spoke of the quiet comfort I carried: that he knew. He knew how much I loved him. He knew, without doubt, that I honoured him, adored him, and that my absence was not a measure of my love.

He went knowing he was loved, and I live knowing he loved me—and in that, I found my peace.

Stella kept me updated on how it all unfolded. She told me how beautifully they celebrated his life. The Bazukufu gave him a grand farewell, full of reverence and joy, commending him to the One he loved above all. Their voices rose in Tukutendereza, that enduring revival anthem, lifting a sound of praise that bridged time, earth, and eternity. He had indeed "fought a good fight, finished [his] course, [and] kept the faith" (2 Timothy 4:7, KJV). He was laid to rest on 9 October, Uganda's Independence Day—a day symbolising national freedom—yet his freedom was of a far higher order. He had already entered the truest liberty: the freedom only Christ can give, the freedom of the redeemed. There was a quiet profundity in that timing, as if his final homegoing reflected the liberty he had long embraced in spirit.

Even in my absence, the love of friends stood in the chasm—filling the void with a kind of grace that defies ordinary measure. It was not the loud kind of love, but a steadfast, embodied presence—an unspoken ministry of consolation. Some were simply there, silent sentinels of sorrow, shouldering a portion of my grief with reverence. Many had known him personally, had visited my family home when he was there. He had welcomed them not only with warmth but with a question he never failed to ask: "*Walokoka? Are you born again?*" It was never rhetorical. He rarely waited for an answer before launching into a fervent witness of Jesus—the One who had transformed his own life, and who, he believed, could transform anyone's. To him, no conversation was too casual for the gospel; every moment was an opportunity for redemption.

Yet it was not only those who knew him who showed up in love. Beatrice had never met him. She had never been to Uganda. And yet, she travelled all the way from Kenya to a foreign land—to bury the father of a friend she had never met. That is love in its most unadulterated form: selfless, sacrificial, uncalculating.

Then there was Dr Doreen—a steady, generous soul who became a pillar in his final days. At the Uganda Heart Institute in Mulago Hospital, where he spent months grappling with a relentless heart condition, she stood beside my family like kin. My mother often spoke of her with teary-eyed gratitude, saying, *"Your friends are treasures."* Her words bore the weight of lived experience—recognising in my friends the very answers to whispered prayers.

And like David, I did not bury our beloved. But I mourned him with everything I had.

In the midst of that darkness, I came to see the quiet beauty of human compassion. In Melbourne, both familiar faces and near strangers gathered around me, offering what comfort they could. Their presence, their words, and even their silences became a balm to my fractured spirit. Grief is a weight too vast to carry alone, but their kindness enfolded me—like a mantle shielding me from the unbearable. They stood beside me in unexpected ways, showing up not just in speech but in stillness. Their love became the hands that held my breaking heart.

But even in the comfort of their presence, a deeper truth settled in—one I could neither escape nor undo.

I would never hear his voice on the other end of the line again. Never see that smile—the one that illuminated my world with its quiet radiance. Never again feel the warmth of his benediction, that profound reassurance that I was brilliant, resilient, beautiful, discerning, and worthy. He perceived me in ways I often struggled to perceive myself. And now, that steadfast witness to my life was no longer here—at least not in body. Yet he would live on, undimmed, in memory.

On my last visit to bid him farewell, I knew deep down there was a chance I might never see him alive again. But knowing is different from believing. I held onto hope, convincing myself that there would be one more or many more visits, more conversations, more embraces and celebration perhaps of all that I would achieve in the faraway land I was going to. And yet, that was it, it was the last time. The last hug. The last moment before a lifetime of longing. But if there is any solace in this, it is the certainty that he knew—he knew I loved him deeply. And I still do. In life, in death, in every breath I take.

In the depths of this sorrow, God was closer, with every step. Every comforting word, every shoulder offered, every small act of kindness was evidence of his presence. Though the pain of losing my father would never truly leave or fade, I pressed on, knowing that somehow, a greater purpose was unfolding—even if for now, I could only see through the veil of tears.

I continued with my course while navigating the uncertainties of accommodation. As I've said before, I deeply acknowledge the immense support asylum seekers receive in Australia, but none compared to the work of the Asylum Seeker Resource Centre (ASRC). Without their assistance, my journey would have been exponentially more difficult, and homelessness would have been a stark reality.

One of their most impactful initiatives was the Rooms for Asylum Seekers project, where individuals with extra space in their homes offered to host an asylum seeker for three months, rent-free. I would be responsible for my food costs, but as a member of the ASRC, I had access to their member's pantry, allowing me to obtain groceries, fresh vegetables, fruits, and toiletries every week.

Additionally, there was a fortnightly free clothing service. I could also visit the General Access Program (GAP) station to communicate any specific needs, and the team would do their utmost to assist—sometimes through practical support, other times by providing vouchers to help bridge those needs.

I still remember the project lead, Skye—her passion for the initiative was palpable. I first met her through GAP, where she introduced the idea to me. At the time, I was still staying at Urban Central, a bustling city backpackers' hostel in Southbank. The prospect she presented was both promising and daunting. Many asylum seekers hesitated to take that step, as it required surrendering the last vestiges of independent living—adjusting to someone else's home, their rules, their rhythms. There's a particular disquiet that comes with such a shift, a quiet erosion of one's sense of autonomy. It feels, in some ways, like your agency is slowly slipping through your fingers.

But when you're hemmed in by circumstance, with few viable paths forward, an opportunity like this can be life-changing. Who knows what doors might open, what unseen blessings might unfold? Sometimes, the greatest gifts don't arrive wrapped in glitter and ribbons. Sometimes, they come quietly—disguised as inconvenience, uncertainty, or surrender. And guided by my faith, I recognised this as a blessing in disguise.

So, I said yes.

Within days, I was matched with my hosts, Simon and Sarah, in Coburg. The arrangement was straightforward: I would stay for three months with all bills covered. After that, my situation would be reassessed, and if needed, I could be placed with another host. My prayer was simple yet urgent—to find stability, to stand on my own feet, and to never feel like a burden or a perennial recipient of charity.

SIMON AND SARAH

I first met Simon and Sarah one afternoon at ASRC. Introductions were made, and plans were set in motion for my transition from Urban Central. Simon would pick me up himself, sparing me the worry of figuring out how to get there. Sarah, however, wouldn't be around, as she was travelling to South America for the next three months. And so, on a late October or early November evening—though I can't recall the exact date, I can replay it vividly in my mind—Simon arrived and took me to their home. For the next three months, this would be my place of refuge as I continued figuring life out: finishing my course, securing a placement, seeking work, and ultimately finding long-term accommodation. Would I need another three months with a different host? That was a question for later. For now, I didn't have to worry about weekly accommodation, rent, or bills. Look at God! Look at this generosity! He was there—still—working things out for me.

For those who declined the Rooms for Asylum Seekers offer, life became significantly harder. The ASRC and HomeGround could only cover accommodation for a limited time, and after three months, support ceased to be classified as crisis accommodation. They were left to navigate a system where referrals to other services often led to dead ends. I knew this firsthand, as week after week we met at the ASRC food bank, and they shared how difficult things had become. Organisations like the Red Cross required extensive proof of financial hardship—bank statements, official documentation—before approving payments under the SRSS program. The Status Resolution Support Services (SRSS) program offers financial aid and casework support to individuals living in Australia while they await a decision on their application for a Protection Visa. However, accessing this support can be daunting, entangled in complex eligibility criteria and rigorous documentation demands.

But when you're already drowning, bureaucracy feels like yet another tide dragging you under. I knew it was God's hand that carried me through it all. Provision, open doors, kindness in unexpected places—these were quiet markers of grace, evidence that even in the fog of unpredictability, He was still scripting my destiny.

Living with Simon was effortless—it felt like a haven far removed from the impersonal confines of Urban Central. It was safe, serene, and mercifully free from stifling regulations. I had a room in their elegant two-bedroom apartment, complete with Wi-Fi that kept me tethered to home and in touch with my children.

Simon took a genuine interest in me—my family, culture, and situation. He engaged deeply, not out of politeness but from a place of authentic empathy. Our conversations often traversed the political instability and economic upheaval back home, the intricacies of my case, and upcoming appointments. He was more than a host—he became a gracious presence whose quiet solidarity buoyed my spirit during an otherwise tumultuous season.

I hadn't been living there long when Julia arrived in Australia to pursue her master's degree in law. She arrived at Simon and Sarah's house on her birthday. Julia was the girlfriend of Simon's best friend, Benni, and the three of them had known each other well for years, long before coming to Australia, back in Germany. I remember the day Julia arrived. Her presence brought more sunshine into the house. She had a beautiful, bold, and friendly personality, with contagious laughter and a warmth in her eyes that made everyone feel at ease. Her curiosity about me, paired with my interest in getting to know her, quickly sparked a friendship. Julia stayed for a little while before finding accommodation nearby, as I had taken over the room she might have occupied during her studies in Australia. Despite this, we remained close and saw each other often.

Just before Christmas, Benni travelled to spend the holiday with Julia and Simon. The reunion was filled with joy—they were so happy to see each other again. The day he arrived, they spent hours catching up, reminiscing about home, family, parents, and mutual friends. The house felt alive, filled with warmth and laughter.

Simon asked if I'd like to invite a friend over for Christmas Eve, so I invited Mahlet. The next day, the boys took charge of preparing the famous stuffed turkey—it turned into a feast to remember! The night was full of laughter, warmth, and the joy of the season.

One of the most touching moments was when Simon gave me a gift from his mother—a beautifully wrapped present with a heartfelt card. Inside was a colourful scarf, a thoughtful gesture that meant so much. I still treasure it—not just as a gift, but as a reminder of that special Christmas, filled with love, hope, and friendship.

On Christmas Day, we went to the beach, spending the day in the sun and enjoying each other's company. It was the perfect way to end the holiday. As I watched the tide roll in and out, I felt deeply grateful—I hadn't spent my first Christmas in Australia alone.

The days between Boxing Day and New Year's always feel like a blur—slow, aimless, and adrift. Who really remembers them? They exist in a strange in-between, where time drifts without urgency, waiting for the year to turn. I spent those days at home, lounging and letting the hours blend together—often on long calls with my children, my mother, and friends back home. Their voices, warm and familiar, reached across the distance like lifelines, tying me to a place that felt far away, but would always be home.

And just like that, 2014 came to an end. A year that didn't simply pass—it happened to me. A year of breaking and rebuilding. Of pain and partings I never imagined I'd have to face, let alone survive. And yet, somehow, I did. It was also a year of firsts—of crossing into the unknown, learning to walk in a life that didn't quite fit yet. A new world. A new country. A new version of me. Australia still felt foreign, but I was determined to make it mine.

Looking back on those 365 days, I saw not just struggle, but resilience. I completed 120 hours of placement at Twin Parks Aged Care Home in Reservoir—an experience that challenged me in ways I hadn't anticipated. With that, I earned a certificate in Aged Care from GuideStar Training Institute: a fresh start, a new path.

Stepping into the job market felt like cruel déjà vu—like being a recent graduate all over again, desperate for an opportunity, but now with so much more at stake. I've always found it ironic—almost absurd—how employers demand experience. Experience, experience, experience. As if it magically appears out of thin air. But where am I supposed to get it if no one will give me the chance?

There was no time to throw a pity party over that frustration—2015 had arrived with one non-negotiable mission: find a job. Bills weren't going to pay themselves, and as far as you know me by now, I wasn't on the list for a billionaire's inheritance.

Before I could add an address to my resume, my peripatetic life barged in like an uninvited guest crashing a wedding. My time in Coburg was over, and once again, I found myself packing my belongings, ready to move. This time, it was Watsonia, where new hosts awaited me—another unfamiliar home, another chapter to be written in this ongoing saga. At this rate, I might as well be the star of a documentary titled *The Asylum Seeker Chronicles: Packing, Unpacking, and Pretending You're Settling In*.

Yet, something about this move felt different. Maybe it was the fresh promise of a new year, or perhaps sheer exhaustion—surely fate had to throw me a bone sooner or later. Maybe it was that familiar January feeling when we convince ourselves we've hit the reset button and that everything will finally fall into place. I wasn't sure if it was a gut feeling or just New Year's optimism, but for the first time in a long while, I sensed that, against all odds, I was starting to find my way.

By the end of January, I had settled into Watsonia, my home for the next three months—the usual hosting period for asylum seekers.

TRISH AND WALTER

Trish and Walter were in their later years, long retired from formal employment but far from idle. Their days were filled with purpose, devoted to community service and social justice causes they held dear. They were humanists at heart—champions of the overlooked, voices for the unheard. Their compassion knew no bounds, and from the moment I stepped into their home, I was enveloped in a warmth that bore a striking resemblance to the embrace of my parents.

They had set aside a private ensuite room for me—comfortable, well-equipped, and thoughtfully prepared. It wasn't just a place to sleep; it was a sanctuary amid the chaos of my life's transition. Living with them felt less like lodging with strangers and more like a long-awaited reunion with family.

Watsonia itself was quiet, nestled away from the city's fast-paced hum, but it had its conveniences. The train station was just a five-minute walk away, ensuring that even though I was far from Melbourne's heart, I was never truly disconnected. And that was important because my days were anything but still. My schedule revolved around job hunting, immigration appointments, and the endless duties of rebuilding life from scratch.

Despite their busy commitments, Trish and Walter made time for shared moments that softened the edges of my reality. We had meals together, and on days I was home, we'd enjoy afternoon tea—simple rituals that spoke volumes about care and inclusion. Each morning before I stepped out, Walter would press a glass of freshly squeezed juice into my hands, a silent yet profound gesture of encouragement.

Their steady belief in my potential helped me regain my balance. On 12 February 2015—barely a week after arriving in Watsonia—I secured my first job in Australia. It felt like the tide was beginning to turn, a gentle but certain sign that I was heading in the right direction. A tangible testament to the power of perseverance and grace—one I'll return to later—but for now, it was enough to feel the first stirrings of hope.

Meanwhile, my immigration application sat in the background, stagnant. I had to perfect the art of waiting and waiting without answers, without movement. It was an exercise in patience, a quiet battle against the unknown.

Yet, even during this season when doubt was a constant voice I had to actively silence, I held onto one truth: the year had begun with favour. The kindness of strangers had become the bridge to possibility, and though I was still navigating the in-between, I was not alone.

Trish and Walter were more than kind—they were a rare kind of generous. Not just in what they said, but in how they lived, in the spaces they cultivated, and in the warmth they extended without hesitation.

From the moment I arrived, they didn't just welcome me—they integrated me into their world. They introduced me to their family, both immediate and extended, weaving me into the fabric of their lives with an ease that made me feel like I had always belonged. Their friends, acquaintances, and the wider community they were part of became familiar faces to me. I wasn't just a guest in their home; I was part of their lives, their conversations, their causes.

But their kindness didn't stop at making me feel included. They stretched their generosity beyond borders, reaching to my children back in Uganda. I remember the moment they told me they had put together a care package—clothes and little necessities carefully chosen with love. They posted it off, and by the grace of timing, it arrived just a few weeks before Easter 2015. I can still picture my children receiving that package, their excitement, their joy. It was a kindness I could never repay.

At the time, both Trish and Walter were deeply involved with the Asylum Seeker Resource Centre. Trish, a retired nurse, volunteered in the ASRC health clinic, tending to those who had been battered by the weight of displacement, offering care with the same tenderness she showed at home. Walter, on the other hand, dedicated his time to teaching English to newly arrived asylum seekers and refugees from non-English speaking backgrounds. He had a patient, unwavering spirit, the kind that made people believe they could find their voice in a foreign land.

Our dinner table conversations often reflected the heart of their work. Tony Abbott was prime minister at the time, and every evening, the news would bring another wave of frustration, sadness, and indignation. ABC News and SBS broadcasts filled our home, unpacking the reality of Australia's refugee policies under the Liberal government. The cruelty embedded in the system—detention centres, border security crackdowns, the relentless dehumanisation of asylum seekers—was not just a political issue to Trish and Walter. It was personal. It was a fight they were engaged in daily.

And then, there was that one morning. A memory I will carry with me for the rest of my life.

I sat with Trish and Walter, listening to the news as the fate of Andrew Chan and Myuran Sukumaran was being discussed with a kind of cold inevitability. Two of the "Bali Nine," a group of Australians convicted in 2005 for attempting to smuggle heroin out of Indonesia, were facing execution. We had followed their story for months, watched as they transformed themselves in prison—Andrew becoming a pastor, Myuran an artist, both dedicating their lives to mentoring fellow inmates. They had repented and changed, and yet, the world refused to show them mercy.

On April 29, 2015, the news broke. They had been executed by firing squad.

The grief that hit me was unexpected and visceral. It wasn't just sadness—it was anger, helplessness, a deep sense of injustice that clawed at my chest. I mourned for them, for their families, for their parents who had fought so hard to save them. I remember reading everything I could about their lives, grasping for some explanation, some justification. But nothing made sense. Who gave humans the right to determine the fate of others in such a final, irreversible way? What kind of world were we living in where redemption wasn't enough?

I remember watching Julie Bishop, the Foreign Minister at the time, deliver a response. Her words were polished and diplomatic—perhaps just as one would expect in such a role—but for me, they felt distant. They didn't offer comfort or help me make sense of the sorrow that lingered quietly in the background. I don't know how others processed it, but for me, that moment left a quiet imprint. It deepened my awareness of how decisions are made, how power is exercised, and how, at times, the humanity behind policies can feel lost in translation. It didn't spark anger, just a quiet awakening—a realisation that justice and compassion don't always walk hand in hand in the world of governance.

Living with Trish and Walter was more than just having a place to stay—it was an education. Through them, I was introduced to Australian politics in a way I had never expected. I learned about the Federation, the division of power between the federal government and the states and territories, the major political parties, and the invisible strings pulling policy decisions behind the scenes. I discovered the difference between ABC and SBS versus the commercial channels—7, 9, and 10—and found myself hooked on programs like *Insight*, captivated by the honesty of the discussions and the complexity of the issues they tackled.

Time moved quickly, and the three-month hosting period in Watsonia drew to a close. Now that I had a job—modest in hours, but meaningful in purpose—I needed to find a more permanent place to live. Another chapter was waiting to unfold.

Joseph, ever dependable, came to my rescue again. He knew someone renting out a room in Footscray and kindly spoke to them on my behalf. Because they trusted him—he'd lived there briefly—they agreed to take me in. And just like that, I moved to Titch Street.

It was shared accommodation, but it gave me my own room, manageable bills, and, most importantly, a sense of independence. Trish and Walter, ever generous, made sure I had the essentials to begin this new phase of life. It felt a bit like a child moving out of home—except this home had been built not by biology, but by pure kindness. During my first week, they prepared meals and delivered them to me, checking in to make sure I was okay. I was loved. I was spoiled. I was being cared for.

Trish and Walter, to this day, are like parents to me. Their care never stopped. I became part of their family—forever woven into the warmth they so freely gave.

Looking back now, those six months within the Rooms for Asylum Seekers project were nothing short of transformative.

I had lived in two homes, each unique, but both rich in kindness and generosity. The project itself was a lifeline—not just because it offered shelter, but because it gave me dignity, stability, and community during one of the most uncertain seasons of my life. It reminded me that even in a foreign land, one could find refuge not just in walls, but in people. Each connection deepened my sense of belonging and broadened my understanding of the community around me. These relationships have lasted far beyond those early days; they remain an important part of my life this day.

THE UNCONVENTIONAL ROAD TO BSL

My journey to landing a job at the Brotherhood of St. Laurence (BSL) was anything but conventional. It wasn't a case of applying, interviewing, and securing a neat little contract. No, mine was a winding road paved with introductions, kindness, and a fair bit of let's just see what happens.

The Brotherhood of St. Laurence is an organisation deeply committed to tackling poverty and disadvantage across Australia. Their work spans everything from supporting vulnerable communities to advocating for social justice and equality—always grounded in compassion and practical support. It was their mission that first drew me to them, but it was the people within BSL who truly made a lasting impact.

It all began when I signed up to be assisted by *Given the Chance*, a BSL program designed to help job seekers—particularly migrants and refugees—find meaningful employment. The name alone felt poetic, because truly, that's what most of us needed: a chance.

Under the guidance of Ahmed Raza, the employment coordinator, I worked tirelessly on my résumé, refining every line as though it were a masterpiece in the making. Ahmed, always an encourager, shared his own immigration journey with me, reminding me that every struggle has an expiry date.

"One day, things will fall into place," he assured me. "Better days are coming. It doesn't feel like it now, but one day, everything will fall into place."

Ahmed then introduced me to Brian, the jobs engagement coordinator, who connected me to Robyn Fuller, the manager of Sumner House, a BSL aged care home in Fitzroy, just a stone's throw from BSL's head office. Robyn's warmth was immediate; she was the type of person who listened with her whole heart. When we met, she asked me to tell my story. I spoke honestly, and I could see how deeply it moved her. Compassion flickered across her face as she absorbed every detail.

"There's no vacancy for a personal care assistant at the moment," she said, her voice heavy with genuine regret. "But—" (Ah, the magic of that word!) "We could use some extra hands in the laundry and the kitchen. And who knows? Maybe something will open up soon."

I didn't hesitate. A foot in the door was all I needed.

Robyn was a firm believer that everyone should be trained in all aspects of service, ensuring that if there was ever a gap, staff could step in seamlessly. It made perfect sense—even if it meant I was about to learn skills I never thought I'd need.

And so began my crash course: *Kitchen Chaos to Laundry Lessons.*

Let me tell you—aged care kitchens don't have slow days. The routine was a relentless cycle: breakfast preparation, serving, and cleaning, followed immediately by morning tea, then lunch, afternoon tea, and supper. It felt like being on a reality cooking show where the contestants never got to sit down.

I quickly discovered that making sandwiches wasn't just about slapping bread together—oh no, there was an art to it. And breakfast? Every resident had their unique preference and getting it wrong was not an option. My coworkers—Bejhinda and Kim in the mornings, and Selima in the evenings—moved with the efficiency of seasoned professionals. They had mastered the rhythm of the kitchen like a well-rehearsed orchestra. I, on the other hand, spent my first few days feeling like I was one order away from disaster.

On the days I wasn't in the kitchen, I was under the strict yet meticulous guidance of Ms Fanny in the laundry. Now, if you think laundry is just about washing and folding, think again. Ms Fanny had a system—a fast, flawless rhythm honed by years of practice. Folding clothes, I assumed, would be the easy part. But no. There was a method to everything: shirts, T-shirts, jumpers, socks—each had its folding style and sequence. And it didn't end there. Each item had to be sorted according to the resident's room and placed neatly into their wardrobe. No shortcuts. No guessing.

But my greatest triumph came when she taught me the elusive skill that many have tried and failed to master: folding a fitted sheet.

I had conquered many things in life, but this? This felt like mastering an ancient and sacred craft. Even now, whenever I see someone wrestling with a fitted sheet like they're trying to tame an unruly beast, I smile to myself, knowing I hold a secret power they do not.

It was in that laundry room, tucked between piles of linen and the hum of machines, that I began to understand something deeper. Mastery is not always found in grand achievements—it can also live in the quiet pride of a perfectly folded sheet, the dignity of care behind a pressed shirt, and the humility of serving behind the scenes. It was there, in the hidden corners of service, that I discovered a grace I didn't know I was looking for.

After about a month, I'd settled into life at Sumner House. I knew the staff, the carers, and the residents by name—and their daily routines too. I had finally "graduated" to personal care work and started getting shifts on the floor. At first, they were small—mostly during the busiest times: mornings from 7:00 AM to 11:30 AM, and then again in the evenings from 4:30 PM to 8:30 PM, covering dinner and bedtime.

Between those shifts, I was in a kind of limbo. Watsonia was too far to go home, so I stayed at the facility. I spent those hours chatting with residents, hearing their stories, catching glimpses of lives that stretched across generations or wandered the city streets. Sometimes, I'd watch buskers perform outside Bourke Street Mall. Tram 86 became my quiet companion, carrying me into the city's pulse whenever I needed to escape the noise inside my own head.

Working in aged care shifts your perspective on life—on mortality, health, and the graceful or painful process of ageing. Some residents reminded me of my parents, my grandparents—pieces of home wrapped in new faces. As their faces became familiar, their presence became a quiet comfort in my otherwise uncertain world. Over time, my hours increased, and eventually, I moved from casual to part-time permanent. It wasn't glamorous, it wasn't easy, but as we say in my language: slowly but surely, the snail made it to the well.

Amid all this steady progress—secure work, growing confidence, a semblance of routine—there was a silent storm always brewing in the background: my immigration case. It was like living with an unpredictable shadow, always hovering just behind me, whispering reminders that no matter how much I tried to build a life here, it could all be taken away with one letter, one decision, one turn of fate.

And then, in early 2016, that letter arrived. My application had been declined.

It was the kind of news that knocked the air out of your lungs. For a few moments, I just sat there, numb. The thought of not seeing my children for the foreseeable future hit like a punch to the gut. The exhaustion, the sacrifices, the endless waiting—it had all led to this? But if life had taught me anything, it was that despair, no matter how justified, had no power to change reality. Immigration wasn't going to have a change of heart just because I was heartbroken. So, after a brief and understandable descent into a mental ditch, I did what I had always done—I fought back.

I filed an appeal with the tribunal and began to strategise. If one door closed, I was determined to find another way. My mind became a battlefield of ideas—a constant tug-of-war between faith and fear. I spent hours on trains and trams, lost in thought so often that I'd sometimes miss my stop. My mind raced with plans and possibilities, while eating and sleeping became harder to prioritise.

There was no clear roadmap, no guaranteed solution—only sheer determination, fuelled by my faith in God's promises, my love for my children, and an unshakable refusal to let circumstances decide our fate. When my thoughts became overwhelming and chaotic, I turned to worship music, repeating the words like declarations. I knew the God who had brought me here would surely bring my children too. I called on the God of my parents—the same God my father had asked to bless me in this land.

BEYOND THE IMPOSSIBLE

And then, on November 29, 2016, something extraordinary happened.

My children arrived in Australia.

Their journey was nothing short of miraculous—an unfolding that defied every logical expectation or explanation. It was a story that lived outside the borders of what was reasonable, something that couldn't be captured in a single sitting or conversation. By all accounts, it shouldn't have been possible… but God.

This tale, even now, feels like something out of a novel. Events unfolded in ways so hard to believe, they stretch the limits of imagination. It's a narrative full of unexpected turns, where things didn't go as one might have hoped. Yet, through it all, strings of hope remained—unyielding and refusing to break.

Yes, there were nights when fear pressed against my chest so tightly, I could barely breathe. Yes, I was afraid of how it would all turn out. How could I not be? The stakes were everything.

But my faith was louder than my fear.

I refused to let fear be the final voice.

Every prayer, every whispered hope, every stubborn act of believing when there was no evidence to believe—it was all built on sheer faith and relentless hope. Their path to join me felt like a dream far beyond my grasp, a vision blurred by impossibility. And yet, I held on.

Because if life teaches you anything, it's this: never underestimate the power of hope.

And then came the odds that stacked higher and higher against us—immigration battles that drained the spirit, endless paperwork that seemed designed to break me, and legal obstacles that threatened to undo it all. Each step forward felt like one step into an even deeper unknown. Each step felt like crossing a minefield, each victory snatched at a price. It was chaotic, bizarre, and often cruel.

One day, perhaps, they will tell their own story—the way they saw it through their young eyes and experienced it. The waiting, the longing, the battles fought on their behalf. Each version will carry its truth.

But for me, the moment I finally held them in my arms again—together, real, breathing the same air—I crumbled. My heart, clenched for so long, finally let go. Tears of relief streamed down my face, carrying years of fear, longing, and silent prayers. The weight of the battle lifted, if only for a moment.

In the softness of their embrace, the world fell away. In that fleeting stillness, I realised that while the fight was far from over, we had crossed a threshold. We had made it.

I knew the war wasn't over. No, it was only just beginning.

But in that moment, the fight felt worth it.

Having them within reach, no longer scattered across oceans, meant everything.

We had won a major battle.

And that night, for the first time in what felt like forever, hope didn't just flicker—it blazed.

It lit up the darkness like the first light of dawn breaking after a long, night.

It reminded me that miracles, no matter how battered they arrive, are still miracles all the same.

Sometimes, the impossible is only a question of timing, and God's timing has a way of turning the unthinkable into the undeniable.

At the same time, another storm was gathering—this time, at work.

Robyn, my manager—the one who had given me a chance—moved on to district nursing in 2017. In her place came a new manager. Her name? Robin. Spelled differently, but I couldn't shake the irony. The change reminded me of Exodus 1:8 (KJV): "*Now there arose up a new king over Egypt, which knew not Joseph.*"

Robin wasted no time shaking things up. Staff grumbled, residents were unsettled, and as expected, resistance brewed. Nobody likes change, and when it's sudden, unexplained, and relentless, it breeds uncertainty. One by one, some of the longtime staff members left. Even worse, some residents passed away, leaving an eerie emptiness in the air.

Then, just when I thought I had weathered enough storms, the phone rang.

I had just returned from a short holiday in Sydney—a rare moment of respite—and was getting ready for my shift when the call came through. The voice on the other end was detached, almost mechanical.

"Your weekend shifts have been cancelled. Effective immediately. There is no need for extra staff."

Just like that.

No warning. No explanation. No cushion to soften the blow. One minute, I had a routine —a sense of stability, a place that felt safe, a livelihood I had fought so hard to secure. The next, I was staring at my phone, feeling the weight of an entire world collapsing in real time.

I stood there, phone still in hand, my mind scrambling to make sense of it. Was this a mistake? A scheduling error? A miscommunication? But deep down, I already knew. The reality settled over me like a heavy, suffocating fog. This was real. This was happening.

Frustration, anger, worry—all of it crashed over me in waves. How was I supposed to survive this? My three little boys had just arrived, still finding their footing in a foreign land, looking to me for stability. And now, this? How was I supposed to keep going with no sense of security, and no clear next step?

Oh, and let's not forget—I was still locked in an immigration war, one that had only intensified now that my children were here. The fire was raging on all fronts.

But if life had taught me anything, it was this—when one storm passes, another may come, but so will another way forward. I just had to breathe. Just for a minute.

Be still.

And know—God would make a way.

VIVIAN

One of the people who truly made a difference during this challenging period was Vivian. She wasn't just a work colleague; over time, she became one of my closest friends. Through the ups and downs, she stood by me, always empathising with my struggles, understanding my situation, and above all, caring for my wellbeing. At the time, she was covering for the Clinical Care Coordinator, who was on leave, and despite her responsibilities, she found a way to make things easier for me.

Vivian didn't just offer a listening ear—she took action. She managed to organise shifts for me at another BSL aged care facility, Sambell Lodge in Clifton Hill, which gave me a reprieve. Between Sambell Lodge and the remaining shifts at Sumner House, I managed to stay afloat for a while. It was a period of juggling, trying to make ends meet, but Vivian's support made all the difference. Her care was a tangible reminder that even in the toughest times, true friends don't just offer their sympathy—they offer their help.

For three years, from February 2015 to December 2018, my life revolved around shifts at Sumner House and Sambell Lodge. There were days when I felt like I was caught in a never-ending cycle, hoping that something more stable would come along. The trials I faced during that time were relentless, and there were moments when it felt like the weight of it all would break me. But, as life often does, the hardships pushed me in ways I hadn't anticipated.

They forced me to step back, take a breath, and look beyond my immediate struggles. I began to see new opportunities, ones I might have otherwise missed. It was during this challenging time that I realised how much growth can come from hardship if we're willing to look for it.

And that's where Vivian's steadfast—no, *indomitable*—support became a force I didn't even know I needed. She believed in me out loud. "With your attitude," she'd say, half-laughing, "you could survive anywhere, do anything, and probably run the place while you're at it." Her words weren't just flattery—they were fuel. They made me believe that resilience wasn't just something I had—it was something I could build a future on.

A MUSTARD SEED

And so I continued in this new cadence of night shifts, moving between Sumner House and Sambell Lodge. During one of those still nights at Sumner House, I found myself working alongside—yes—another Robyn. An RN this time. I know, it's almost comical at this point. What were the odds? But maybe there *was* something in the spelling. The two I had met who spelled their name Robyn—with a "y"—seemed to carry a quiet discernment, a kind of intuitive intelligence and depth of empathy that had been sorely missing in Robin, the manager who had replaced my first one. Maybe it *was* the "y"—that gentle curve that softened everything.

This Robyn was the seasoned kind of nurse whose presence spoke volumes. She had the dry wit of someone who'd seen it all and the calm capability that only years of real experience could offer. Having worked across countless hospitals, she had now chosen the slower pace of aged care. She often joked—half amused, half sincere—that she felt more at home with the residents than with the chaos of a hospital ward. There was something wonderfully grounded about her, someone who knew what truly mattered after walking through many corridors of life.

That night, as we moved through our routine tasks, our conversation meandered from small talk into something more reflective. She asked about my story, and I shared a little—just enough to give her a sense of where I'd come from and what I'd once studied.

Then she paused, looked at me with thoughtful curiosity, and asked,

"Why haven't you had your degrees assessed?"

Such a simple question. But it landed with unexpected weight. No one had asked me that before—not like that. Not with the kind of quiet conviction that said, *Of course it matters. Of course you matter.*

It reminded me of the first Robyn—the one who had given me my first opportunity in this country. She had opened a door that allowed my foot to step in. And now, this second Robyn, perhaps unknowingly, was nudging me toward the next one.

She said it didn't make sense that I wasn't using my qualifications—especially coming from a Commonwealth country.

"Surely your education is worth something," she said. "Your paperwork doesn't even need translation!"

Her words planted a seed, one that would grow into something far bigger than I ever imagined. Robyn's gentle nudge became the catalyst that set me on a path I hadn't even dared to consider before.

You might wonder—surely it crossed my mind at some point? But when you have so much going on, your focus narrows to just the next step: simply getting by.

At first, I hesitated. Would the process be long? Complicated? Expensive? But Robyn was persistent, and I decided to take her advice. To my surprise, the process was far more straightforward than I had anticipated and free.

A few weeks later, I received the Australian equivalent of my qualifications. Holding that official document in my hands felt like holding a beacon—something that illuminated a path I hadn't dared to fully imagine before. I wanted to frame it, laminate it, carry it with me everywhere as proof that new opportunities were no longer just distant hopes but real, tangible possibilities.

In that moment, the future didn't feel so heavy. It hummed with promise, whispering of chances waiting to be seized, and a journey I could finally face with renewed confidence.

Armed with this validation, I started actively looking for opportunities on BSL's intranet. You see, I had come to love working for the organisation. I loved their mission, their values, and most of all, the fact that they had once taken a chance on me when no one else had. I wanted to grow within BSL, to give back in a more meaningful way.

What followed was a relentless search for suitable internal job opportunities. God loves a trier! It wasn't long before an opportunity appeared—one I thought, perhaps, I could try for.

So, I did.

What came next was an intense, exhausting interview process. There were many steps—each one testing not just my skills, but my endurance. Yet with every interview, and every waiting period, I felt myself inching closer. I kept hoping. I kept praying. I kept believing that somehow, somewhere, breakthrough would find me.

And it did.

On January 8, 2019, the call came. I received the official contract: full-time, permanent employment with BSL. It wasn't just a job offer; it was a turning point. A new beginning.

My official start date was set for January 17, 2019.

The hours were humane: Monday to Friday, 9 AM to 5 PM. No more casual unpredictable rosters that kept me away from my boys. Here, there were Rostered Days Off (RDOs) if I chose to opt in, generous leave entitlements, and even the freedom to request flexible or compressed work arrangements to better fit the shape of my days.

For the first time in a long while, the structure wasn't something I had to fight against—it was something that supported me. I allowed myself to believe that maybe, just maybe, we had turned a corner.

But beyond all the formal benefits, the greatest gift this role gave me was time. Precious, irreplaceable time to care for my boys and to hold together the fragile rhythms of our little household. I had the opportunity to be there when the boys needed me most. Time to attend school events without begging someone to cover my shift. Time to be home for dinners, homework battles, and late-night talks—the small, ordinary moments that quietly stitch a family together.

You see, I was all they had—their only constant, their steady ground. I had pieced together a patchwork family made up of "uncles" and "aunties"—friends who loved us deeply but, like everyone, were busy and stretched thin. Sarah was one of those rare gems. Even after working active night shifts, she would still swing by the ASRC, collect our fortnightly groceries, and drop them off at our apartment on her way home.

Yes, we were still seeking asylum then, and the ASRC became our lifeline. Depending on how many hours of work one could manage, they helped fill in the gaps—especially for families with children. I truly can never put into words what the ASRC meant to me, to us. What would I have done without it? But God knew. All I had to do was trust Him.

Some days, I'd forget to leave the key out for Sarah, and with the boys at school, she'd end up leaving the bags with our neighbour, Mr Asef. We lived in an apartment building that required a key or access code just to get inside. If you didn't plan ahead, your Uber Eats or HelloFresh delivery might be left at the entrance—an open invitation to whoever walked by.

Now, about HelloFresh. The boys had watched so many of those bright, bouncy ads that they pestered me to try it. Eventually, I gave in, and we excitedly ordered a week's supply. But when the box was delivered, it was left outside the building. By the time we realised, it had vanished.

I often wondered if a passerby had taken it as a divine provision—a surprise blessing. Maybe someone out there had prayed for a meal that day, and our HelloFresh box became the answer. Who knows? I just hope they enjoyed it. They probably had a feast that week—on our dime, but maybe by God's design.

But all of that—the missed deliveries, the rushed grocery runs, the improvisations to get by—started to fade away once I found some time for myself. Suddenly, I wasn't in a constant race against the clock. I wasn't losing out on my kids' childhoods, minute by minute and hour by hour. I could actually be there. I could finally breathe.

Walking into that training room on my first day felt like stepping into the sunlight after years of living in grey. It was as if I had trudged through endless winters, and now the sun was finally breaking through the clouds. There was no big celebration, no dramatic moment—just a quiet room filled with friendly faces and the comforting feeling that I didn't have to expect the worst anymore. The atmosphere was filled with the nerves of a first day, shared smiles, and unspoken stories. We were all strangers, yet somehow, we felt a connection in this new beginning. In that calm moment, I discovered a sense of belonging I had been missing for so long.

And deep within me, for the first time in years, something stirred—an ineffable flicker of hope, fragile yet unyielding. It whispered that maybe, just maybe, we were not only going to be okay... but standing at the cusp of becoming something more. A future not merely survived, but lived. A life not patched together in haste, but unfolding—quietly, deliberately—like dawn stretching across a bruised sky.

And perhaps, just perhaps, the next chapter was already reaching for me.

"But as it is written, Eye hath not seen, nor ear heard, neither have entered into the heart of man, the things which God hath prepared for them that love him."
—1 Corinthians 2:9 (KJV)

www.ingramcontent.com/pod-product-compliance
Lightning Source LLC
Chambersburg PA
CBHW071233070526
44583CB00017B/2161